Best of Both
Fact and Fiction Texts

Editing and activities by Kate Oliver
Cover: Blaise Thompson
Chapter title pages: Rebecca Scambler
Printed by: Gutenberg Press
Published by the English and Media Centre, © 2008
ISBN: 978-1-906101-03-9

Thanks to:
Barbara Bleiman, Michael Simons and Lucy Webster for help in finding and selecting the texts.

Fran Stowell and Rebecca Scambler for help with the text.

Kate Chapman & Alison Boardman, Hornsey School for Girls, Laura Knight, Battersea Technology College, Angharad Ryder Owen, Norbury Business and Enterprise College, Nina Rosenzweig, CEA, Islington for advice on the choice of texts.

Penguin Books Ltd for 'Note to Sixth-Grade Self' by Julia Orringer from *How to Breathe Underwater* (2005); 'Chin Up, My Little Angel – Winning is for Losers' by Jeremy Clarkson from *The World According to Clarkson* (2005); The Wylie Agency (UK) Ltd for 'How the Water Feels to the Fishes' by Dave Eggers from *How the Water Feels to the Fishes* (2007); Lucinda Roy and Jean Naggar Literary Agency for 'Seeing Things in the Dark' by Lucinda Roy from *Go Girl! The Black Woman's Book of Travel and Adventure*, ed Elaine Lees (1999); Barbara Bleiman for 'A Perfect Afternoon' (2008); Sebastian Coe and London 2012 for 'My Heroes Were Olympians' (2005); Jerome Monahan and Stuart Pearce for 'The Voice Coach' (2008); Little Brown for 'Treasure's Pocket Money' by Gina Davidson from *Treasure – the Trials of a Teenage Terror* (1993, 1996); 'Tournament' by Matthew Polly from *American Shaolin* (2007); Random House for 'One Woman's Cup of Tea' by Xinran from *What the Chinese Don't Eat* (2006); extracts from *Touching the Void* by Joe Simpson (2003); 'What, Me Worry' from *The Life and Times of the Thunderbolt Kid* by Bill Bryson (2007); Noel K Hannan for 'I Can't Forget the Girl in the Orange Dress' first published in the Guardian, 16/09/06; AP Watt Literary Agency for 'My Polish Teacher's Tie' by Helen Dunmore from *Ice Cream* (2001); Guardian News for 'I Fell Through Arctic Ice' by Gary Rolfe, published in Guardian Weekend magazine (2006); 'The Birthday Cake' by Daniel Lyons from *Birthday Stories* edited by Haruki Murakami (2006); Harper Collins for 'Just Like Your Father' by Jacqueline Wilson, published in *The Family Tree*, ed. Miriam Hodgson (1999); 'Bits of an Autobiography I May Not Write' by Morris Gleitzman from *Kids Night In* (Warchild, 2003); Abner Stein for 'The Emissary' by Ray Bradbury published in *Ghost Stories* ed Robert Westall (2004); David Higham Associates for 'Begi-begi and Jill-jillie' by Farrukh Dhondy from *Like Father, Like Son*, edited by Tony Bradman (2006); Bloomsbury Publishing Plc for 'The Ultimate Safari' by Nadine Gordimer from *Telling Tales* (2004); David Almond for 'Originality' (2006) first published in Teachit Newsletter Copyright © David Almond (UK) Ltd (2006); Writers' Tips published on www.storiesontheweb.org, Birmingham Libraries; Telegraph Syndication for 'Who Let the Dogs Out?' By Nic Fleming, published in *The Daily Telegraph* (05/04/2004); 'Be a 'Bad' Parent' by Alice Thomson, first published in *The Daily Telegraph* (06/06/2007); BBC News Online for 'Cameras Show Who Let the Dogs Out', published BBC News Online (04/10/04); Walker Books for *Bat Loves the Night* by Nicola Davies, illus by Sarah Fox-Davies (2001, 2002); BBC for 'Children 'Scared' to Play Outside', CBBC Newsround website (03/08/2005); Excerpt taken from *Worst-Case Scenario Survival Handbook* by Joshua Piven (2005). Permission granted by Quirk Productions, Inc. Play England for 'Playday 2008 – Give Us a Go' and an ICM survey commissioned by Play England for Playday (2007); Profile Books and *New Scientist* for 'Last Words' from *Does Anything Eat Wasps?* ed. Mick O'Hare © *New Scientist* (2005)

Contents

Introduction

Best of Both is a rich collection of contemporary fiction and non-fiction in the spirit of the new Programme of Study for English and the renewed Framework for Teaching English. The collection is aimed mainly at KS3 but has plenty to offer at GCSE too.

How the Collection is Organised

The texts are organised in thematic chapters. Each chapter includes different types of writing and texts for a range of abilities, including some extension work. However, the chapters also become progressively more challenging, with 'Playing Out' being the most accessible and 'A Question of Sport' the most demanding. Newspaper articles are not laid out as such, but, where possible, a thumbnail of the article as it originally appeared is included at the end of the text, should you wish to discuss layout. Words and phrases which may not appear in a classroom dictionary have been glossed for your reference. Contextual information has been given for texts where appropriate. Where a text was originally published in America, American spelling has been retained. Descriptions of text types can be found on pages 236-239.

Using the Collection

There are ideas for activities on each text, as well as for comparative work across each chapter. The texts and activities could be used in various ways, for example:

- – a single text could be used as a one-off lesson
- – one or more texts could be incorporated into an existing scheme of work
- – a chapter could be treated as a thematic unit
- – work could range across chapters, for example looking at a particular type of writing. Some ideas are given below.

Be aware that a few of the texts contain some strong language or challenging content. Please read the texts thoroughly before deciding whether they are suitable for your class.

Some Ideas for Work Ranging Across the Collection

Playing Out

What, Me Worry?

The only time I have ever broken a bone was also the first time I noticed that adults are not entirely to be counted on. I was four years old and playing on Arthur Bergen's jungle gym when I fell off and broke my leg.

Arthur Bergen lived up the street, but was at the dentist or something when I called, so I decided to have a twirl on his new jungle gym before heading back home.

I don't remember anything at all about the fall, but I do remember very clearly lying on damp earth, the jungle gym now above and around me and seeming awfully large and menacing all of a sudden, and not being able to move my right leg. I remember also lifting my head and looking down my body to my leg which was bent at an unusual – indeed, an entirely novel – angle. I began to call steadily for help, in a variety of tones, but no one heard. Eventually I gave up and dozed a little.

At some point I opened my eyes and a man with a uniform and a peaked cap was looking down at me. The sun was directly behind him so I couldn't see his face; it was just a hatted darkness inside a halo of intense light.

'You all right, kid?' he said.

'I've hurt my leg.'

He considered this for a minute. 'You wanna get your mom to put some ice on it. Do you know some people named…'– he consulted a clipboard –' …Maholovich?'

'No.'

He glanced at the clipboard again. 'A. J. Maholovich. 3725 Elmwood Drive.'

'No.'

'Doesn't ring a bell at all?'

'No.'

'This is Elmwood Drive?'

'Yes.'

'OK, kid, thanks.'

'It really hurts,' I said. But he was gone.

I slept a little more. After a while Mrs Bergen pulled into their driveway and came up the back steps with bags of groceries.

'You'll catch a chill down there,' she said brightly as she skipped past.

'I've hurt my leg.'

She stopped and considered for a moment. 'Better get up and walk around on it. That's the best thing. Oh, there's the phone.' She hurried into the house.

I waited for her to come back but she didn't. 'Hello,' I croaked weakly now. 'Help.'

Bergen's little sister, who was small and therefore stupid and unreliable, came and had a critical look at me.

'Go and get your mom,' I said. 'I'm hurt.'

She looked at my leg with comprehension if not compassion. 'Owie,' she said.

'Yes, owie. It really hurts.'

She wandered off, saying, 'Owie, owie,' but evidently took my case no further.

Mrs Bergen came out after some time with a load of washing to hang.

'You must really like it down there,' she chuckled.

'Mrs Bergen, I think I've really hurt my leg.'

'On that little jungle gym?' she said, with good-natured scepticism, but came closer to look at me. 'I don't think so, honey.' And then abruptly: 'Christamighty! Your leg! It's backwards!'

'It hurts.'

'I bet it does, I bet it does. You wait right there.'

She went off.

Eventually, after quite some time, Mr Bergen and my parents pulled up in their respective cars at more or less the same moment. Mr Bergen was a lawyer. I could hear him talking to them about liability as they came up the steps. Mr Bergen was the first to reach me.

'Now you do understand, Billy, that technically you were trespassing...'

They took me to a young Cuban doctor on Woodland Avenue and he was in a panic. He started making exactly the kind of noises Desi Arnaz made in *I Love Lucy* when Lucy did something really bone-headed – only he was doing this over my leg. 'I don' thin' I can do this,' he said, and looked at them beseechingly. 'It's a really bad break. I mean look at it. Wow.'

I expect he was afraid he would be sent back to Cuba. Eventually he was prevailed upon to set the break. For the next six weeks my leg remained more or less backwards. The moment they cut off the cast, the leg spun back into position and everyone was pleasantly surprised. The doctor beamed. 'Tha's a bit of luck!' he said happily.

Then I stood up and fell over.

'Oh,' the doctor said and looked troubled again. 'Tha's not good, is it?'

He thought for a minute and told my parents to take me home and to keep me off the leg for the rest of the day and overnight and see how it was in the morning.

'Do you think it will be all right then?' asked my father.

'I've no idea,' said the doctor.

The next morning I got up and stepped gingerly on to my wounded leg. It felt OK. It felt good. I walked around. It was fine. I walked a little more. Yes, it was definitely fine.

I went downstairs to report this good news and found my mother bent over in the laundry room sorting through clothes.

'Hey, Mom, my leg's fine,' I announced. 'I can walk.'

'Oh, that's good, honey,' she said, head in the dryer. 'Now where's that other sock?'

Bill Bryson: The Life and Times of the Thunderbolt Kid (2007)

A Perfect Afternoon

Mummy was busy. She had friends coming to tea. They were new friends and she wanted to impress them, so she was baking a cake. In the kitchen, everything was spread out on the kitchen table – flour, butter, mixing bowls, a carton of eggs and a little trail of sugar leading to a small dollop of half mixed cake. Mummy had her apron on and her face was very pink.

We sat for a while swinging our legs, poking our fingers in the sugar, waiting for her to finish mixing the cake so we could lick out the bowl. Then David stretched his hand that bit too far and tipped over the bottle of milk. Trouble. Mummy's mouth opened. We reckoned it was worth giving up our bowl licking to escape before the yell. So we made a run for it, out the back door, into the garden and on through the gate to the road beyond. **▌▌**

The long afternoon stretched out before us, the usual games in the house now no longer possible with Mummy on the warpath. We decided to try calling for Philippa next door. Older than us, aged 9, we looked up to her and relied on her for ideas. One day she would suggest playing Batman and Robin battling the forces of evil – being the youngest, I was, of course, the forces of evil. The next day she'd rope us into her nearly new sale of old toys on the pavement outside her house. David and her shared out the earnings, giving me a penny or two to quieten my protests. Once we climbed up into the apple tree in her garden, ate the hard little apples, gave ourselves stomachache and ran home to lie on the sofa and be comforted with a hot water bottle and a drink of squash. Sometimes we explored beyond the gardens, edging close to the woods at the end of the road but always holding back from entering it, for fear of the shadows cast by the big old oak trees and the smell of death from the rotting leaves. **▌▌**

This day, we rang the bell but Philippa wasn't in. We hung around, kicking the gravel on the path, angry with her for not being there and wondering what to do without her to tell us. It was a hot afternoon. The sun hanging high in the sky made us sweaty and irritable.

David suggested going over the road to hang around outside the house of that other boy, Peter, the even bigger one, who Philippa sometimes chatted to. I didn't like him.

He sometimes laughed at me. If I wore short socks he laughed at them. If I wore long ones, he laughed at them. He called me 'Girly wurly' and 'Cry baby bunting' and said girls were silly and boys were good at everything. I said I didn't want to play with him. But David always knew best, being eighteen and a half months two weeks three days four and a half hours older than me and a boy, so I didn't say anything. We crossed the road and walked slowly backwards and forwards outside Peter's house, peering into the windows from a distance to see if we might be able to spot him. Finally, a face appeared at the kitchen window. It was his mother. She waved to us. I saw David blushing, as she beckoned us towards the house.

'He's upstairs in his bedroom,' she said as she opened the door.

We wiped our feet on the mat and tiptoed quietly up the stairs, as Mummy would expect us to do in someone else's house. The boy, Peter, was lying on his bed reading a comic. He looked up slowly, as if not in the least bit interested in us.

'Whatya want?' he said.

'Dunno,' said David. 'Wanna play with us?'

'Maybe,' Peter replied after a long pause. 'I'll play with you. But not her. She's a cry baby.'

I felt the tears coming but David shoved me hard and said, 'She's got to come too. Gotta look after her.'

'Awright then. But she'd better not stop us doing things, or cry.'

'You won't will you?' David said, giving me a stern look.

I shook my head.

We trailed downstairs after him, down the path and out onto the road.

'What shall we do?' asked David.

'The woods,' said Peter. 'We'll have an adventure in the woods.'

David looked at me and then away. 'Yeah,' he said. 'Why not?'

'Been in the woods before?' asked Peter.

'Yeah, loads of times,' said David, not looking at me.

'Loads of times,' I said, looking at David.

'Me too,' said Peter, looking down at his shoes.

'Let's go then,' David said and marched off towards the end of the road.

The sun was high in the sky, beating down on us. But as we reached the entrance to the woods, darkness descended and a dank wrapping of mould and moss and leaves made us feel chilly and cut off from home.   ▮

Peter whooped and his voice echoed, bouncing from tree to tree, like the call of an owl. The boys ran through the trees, snapping branches and crackling the crispy leaves under foot. David grabbed a stick and banged it against a fallen log until it broke in two. Peter walked along the log like a tightrope walker, leaping off the end with an almighty yell. David swung from a low hanging branch, shrieking his Tarzan call. I ran after them, making little noises that weren't crying.

Peter and David ran ahead, skimming low under the branches. I ran after them, watching as they tripped through the undergrowth. They were speeding along and I was getting left behind. But all of a sudden they stopped dead. Right in front of them, standing in the bracken, was a man. He was well dressed, in a neat jumper, with a shirt and tie. He wore small round glasses and his hair was brylcreemed down, short and tidy. He said hello.   ▮

'Hello,' said Peter. David followed.

'What about you, little girl?' said the man.

'Hello,' I said very quietly.

'Let's play a little game,' he said.

'What sort of game?' said Peter.

He laughed. 'A game of life and death,' he said.   ▮

David looked towards me. His face was pale and afraid. 'Let's go,' he said.

'Run!' shouted Peter.

In that instant, the two boys turned to run. I noticed that David was crying, tears flooding his face, as he raced past me. And I heard Peter's frightened howls. But I was rooted to the spot. And my eyes were dry. I watched the man. He moved a fraction of an inch toward me. I stood there. I smelt the dark rotting leaves beneath my feet.

He took a blade from his pocket. He looked at it. Its metal was dark in the gloom of the trees.

'Don't worry,' he said quietly. 'It's a game where I die and you live.'

'Tell the grown-ups to come and find me,' he said. 'I've written a letter. So they understand. Tell them where I am.'

I nodded.   ▮

'Now go,' he said.

Slowly I turned. And slowly, carefully, I walked towards the arch of light at the edge of the wood, where I knew I would find my way home.

Out on the road, David and Peter were waiting for me. They were on the other side of the road looking towards the wood. David was wiping his nose on his sleeve. Peter, when he saw me, turned away, hiding his face, blotchy and smeared. I walked over to them. Together, not looking at each other, we retraced our steps, back to Peter's house, where, without a word, he turned up his path, opened the front door and disappeared into his house. David and I walked on silently, towards our own home. We said nothing.

In the kitchen, Mummy was cleaning up the tea and stacking the plates in the sink. The remains of a sponge cake with lemon frosted icing sat on the kitchen table. A cake knife lay beside it, bright and sharp in the late afternoon sun.

Mummy was in a really good mood. Her tea had gone well. She'd had fun.

'Thank goodness you two got out from under my feet! The cake was a dream. There's a piece left for each of you.' She cut two slices and put them on plates. 'All in all, it's been just perfect! A perfect afternoon.'

We sat at the table eating our cake. And we didn't say a thing.

Barbara Bleiman (2008)

Be a 'Bad' Parent and Let Your Children Out

I asked my mother yesterday how much freedom she had as a child. 'Well,' she replied, 'I walked to my nursery school in Cambridge alone, aged three, and by four I was roaming the fields behind my house on my hobby-horse.'

After that, she explained, came the war. 'Your grandfather was away and your grandmother was organising the Women's Voluntary Service; no one knew where the four children were.

'We broke into requisitioned houses and made camps; we spent our afternoons canoeing down the Cam without life-jackets, eating sausages out of tins and, when it rained, we slipped into the cinema to watch unsuitable love stories and horrifying images of the liberation of the concentration camps.

'No one worried about us, they had more important issues on their minds.'

Her childhood sounded idyllic. My mother explained that it wasn't always perfect.

She had once been accosted by a man while bicycling to her friend across the water meadows. 'He tried to force himself on me but I managed to get away. I carried on cycling to my friend's house and ate my tea; it never occurred to me to say anything until I went home.

'The police were called but I was back on my bike the next day.'

My mother took a similar attitude to my childhood.

My younger sister and I were allowed to take the Tube home from school across London every day from the age of five.

My sister was hit by a car once when she crossed a busy road to go to a sweet shop. She broke her leg but, as soon as it had mended, we were walking home alone again.

If we wanted to go to ballet or Brownies, we biked on our Choppers.

It was frightening going under the subways of busy streets when it was dark, but it never occurred to us to ask our parents to drive us to after-school activities.

My brothers took the train to my grandmother's in Suffolk on their own from the age of six and spent all day without adults in the park playing football.

When we moved to the countryside to live we had even more freedom to mess around in boats and with ponies. There was a local flasher, but as long as he didn't scare the ponies, he didn't trouble us.

Now, according to the Good Childhood Inquiry, children have everything – iPods, computer games and designer clothes – except the freedom to play outside on their own.

A poll commissioned as part of the inquiry found that just under half the adults questioned (43 per cent) thought that 14 was the earliest age at which children should be allowed to go out unsupervised.

Two-thirds of 10-year-olds have never been to a shop or the park by themselves.

Fewer than one in 10 eight-year-olds walk to school alone. After the disappearance of Madeleine McCann, we have become even more obsessed with eliminating risk.

I'm just as neurotic as other parents. I walk my three-, four- and six-year-old to school every day, clutching their hands.

Their every moment in London is supervised, with playdates and trips to museums.

I drive them to football and tennis. No wonder they love going to the country where they can spend all day making camps in the garden, pretending to be orphans.

It isn't just because I fear they may be abducted or run over, it's because I'm also worried about being seen as a bad parent.

When I let my eldest son go to the loo on his own on a train, less than 20 foot from where I was seated, the guard lectured me on my irresponsibility.

When we go to the park there are signs in the playground saying that parents may be prosecuted if they leave their children unsupervised, and at the swimming pool (where as children we spent half our holidays dive-bombing each other, without a grown-up in sight) there must now be an adult for every two children.

It is insane. My children still end up in the A & E department as often as we did. The inside of a house can be more dangerous than the street, and sitting at a computer all day, eating crisps, carries more long-term risks than skateboarding alone to a park.

The 'terrifying' outdoors is actually safer than it was 30 years ago. In 1977, 668 children were killed on the roads, either in cars or as pedestrians. That number has now dropped to 166.

The number of children murdered has remained consistent at around 79 murders a year. The number of children who drown in rivers or swimming pools has halved. The only place your child is now more at risk is on a trampoline.

So let your children out: they are less likely to harm themselves bicycling to the swings than they are bouncing up and down in their own back yard.

Alice Thomson: The Daily Telegraph (2007)

Be a 'bad' parent and let your children out

I asked my mother yesterday how much freedom she had as a child. "Well," she replied, "I walked to my nursery school in Cambridge alone, aged three, and by four I was roaming the fields behind my house on my hobby-horse."

After that, she explained, came the war. "Your grandfather was away and your grandmother was organising the Women's Voluntary Service; no one knew where the four children were. We broke into requisitioned houses and made camps; we spent our afternoons canoeing down the Cam without life-jackets, eating sausages out of tins and, when it rained, we slipped into the cinema to watch unsuitable love stories and horrifying images of the liberation of the concentration camps. No one worried about us, they had more important issues on their minds."

Her childhood sounded idyllic. My mother explained that it wasn't always perfect. She had once been accosted by a man while bicycling to her friend across the water meadows. "He tried to force himself on me but I

managed to get away. I carried on cycling to my friend's house and ate my tea; it never occurred to me to say anything until I went home. The police were called but I was back on my bike the next day."

My mother took a similar attitude to my childhood. My younger sister and I were allowed to take the Tube home from school across London every day from the age of five. My sister was hit by a car once when she crossed a busy road to go to a sweet shop. She broke her leg but, as soon as it had mended we were walking home alone again. If we wanted to go to ballet or Brownies, we biked on our Choppers. It was frightening going under the subways of busy streets when it was dark, but it never occurred to us to ask our parents to drive us to after-school activities.

My brothers took the train to my grandmother's in Suffolk on their own from the age of six and spent all day without adults in the park playing football. When we moved to the countryside to live we had even more freedom to

Alice Thomson

mess around in boats and with ponies. There was a local flasher, but as long as he didn't scare the ponies, he didn't trouble us.

Now, according to the Good Childhood Inquiry, children have everything – iPods, computer games and designer clothes – except the freedom to play outside on their own. A poll commissioned as part of the inquiry found that just under half the adults questioned (43 per cent) thought that 14 was the earliest age at which children should be allowed to go out unsupervised. Two-thirds of 10-

year-olds have never been to a shop or the park by themselves. Fewer than one in 10 eight-year-olds walk to school alone. After the disappearance of Madeleine McCann, we have become even more obsessed with eliminating risk.

I'm just as neurotic as other parents. I walk my three-, four- and six-year-old to school every day, clutching their hands. Their every moment in London is supervised, with playdates and trips to museums. I drive them to football and tennis. No wonder they love going to the country where they can spend all day making camps in the garden, pretending to be orphans.

It isn't just because I fear they may be abducted or run over, it's because I'm also worried about being seen as a bad parent. When I let my eldest son go to the loo on his own on a train, less than 20 ft from where I was seated, the guard lectured me on my irresponsibility. When we go to the park there are signs in the playground saying that parents may be prosecuted if they leave their children unsupervised, and

at the swimming pool (where as children we spent half our holidays dive-bombing each other, without a grown-up in sight) there must now be an adult for every two children.

It is insane. My children still end up in the A & E department as often as we did. The inside of a house can be more dangerous than the street, and sitting at a computer all day, eating crisps, carries more long-term risks than skateboarding alone to a park.

The "terrifying" outdoors is actually safer than it was 30 years ago. In 1977, 668 children were killed on the roads, either in cars or as pedestrians. That number has now dropped to 166. The number of children murdered has remained consistent at around 79 murders a year. The number of children who drown in rivers or swimming pools has halved. The only place your child is now more at risk is on a trampoline.

So let your children out: they are less likely to harm themselves bicycling to the swings than they are bouncing up and down in their own back yard.

Children 'Scared' to Play Outside

Children don't play outdoors much because they believe the outside world is not safe, a survey has shown.

Young people said they think the outdoors is dangerous and even if it was safe, there are not enough facilities laid on for them.

More than one in four kids asked said they didn't play outside as much as they'd like to.

'The Playday survey is a wake-up call,' a Children's Society spokeswoman said.

'We must protect children's right to play and ensure every child has access to outdoor public space. Play isn't a luxury,' the spokeswoman added.

The research was carried out to mark national Playday, which takes place on Wednesday, and aims to encourage children to play more, both inside and outside.

Computer games

As well as not feeling safe, young people also said they didn't have enough time to play outside, as there were too many other things going on.

Play experts are worried that kids spend all their time in their bedrooms playing computer games and watching TV, rather than getting fresh air and exercise outside.

Health bosses are also worried about rising obesity levels among children as they don't get enough exercise.

CBBC Newsround website report (2005)

Playday

This text is a leaflet designed to publicise Playday 2008. Playday is an annual celebration of children's right to play.

1 | Playday 2008 – Give us a go!

Playday is the annual celebration of children's right to play - a national campaign, which this year reaches its climax on Wednesday 6 August. On Playday and throughout the summer of 2008, thousands of children, young people and communities will get out and play at hundreds of locally organised events across the UK. Whether this is your first Playday or your twenty-first, what better way to celebrate than by giving children and young people the chance to play at your very own Playday event?

Playday: Give us a go!
As well as being a great opportunity for children and young people to get out and play, Playday provides an opportunity to raise awareness about some serious issues affecting children's play.

This year's Playday theme is *Give us a go!* The campaign promotes the benefits of allowing children to manage their own risks whilst playing and aims to counter the risk-averse 'cotton wool' culture that can limit children's play. We will be calling for children and young people to be allowed challenging and adventurous play opportunities as enjoyed by previous generations before them.

Although Playday reaches its peak on Wednesday 6 August this year, children and young people should benefit from being able to play freely all year round. To ensure this can happen, consider planning a longer-term campaign to follow on from your Playday event. Refer to the section *Developing a campaign* in this guide to give you ideas about developing a local campaign.

Through play, children learn about themselves and the world around them

Through play, children can learn how to manage challenge and risk for themselves in everyday situations

What happens on Playday?

On Playday, and throughout the summer, hundreds of events will take place to celebrate Playday. Celebrations range from small neighbourhood gatherings to large public events organised by local authorities and national organisations. In previous years children have taken over Trafalgar Square, attended jubilee style street parties, and enjoyed large-scale mud pie and den building in parks and village greens.

Play England coordinates the campaign in consultation with a national steering group, which includes representatives from Play Wales, Play Scotland and PlayBoard Northern Ireland as well as other national and regional representatives.

A comprehensive body of research is published to support the Playday campaign; this is available on the Playday website closer to the time. As well as informing the national campaign, the research programme helps to generate interest from both national and local media, which raises the profile of play.

Who can organise a Playday event?

Anyone can organise a Playday event. Big or small, there are lots of different ways to celebrate Playday. Whether it's a large community-wide event or a get-together with friends and family – find the way that suits you!

Playday events are often organised by play associations, local authorities, holiday play schemes, extended schools, children's centres, nurseries, preschool playgroups, residents' associations, community development workers, childminders, or simply someone who lives in locally and wants to give children and young people the opportunity to play there for the day.

The Playday campaign team provide Playday event organisers with lots of resources and advice on delivering a successful day including: this guide, seminars, a dedicated website, telephone helpline, and further materials to help with your event, including posters, promotional items and a template news release. So go on, what's stopping you?

Anyone can organise a Playday event.
So go on, what's stopping you?

This year's theme

This year's Playday campaign is promoting the benefits of allowing children to manage their own risks whilst playing and aims to counter the risk-averse 'cotton wool' culture that can limit children's play.

Under the theme of *Give us a go!* there are some important messages to think about:

• All children need opportunities to take their own risks when playing; they need and want challenge, excitement and uncertainty in play.

• Through play, children can learn how to manage challenge and risk for themselves in everyday situations.

• Opportunities for children to take risks while playing are reducing, as increasingly health and safety considerations are impacting on children's play.

• Adults should provide for children and young people to have adventurous play opportunities.

Play England Survey

Play England conducted this survey as part of the Good Childhood Inquiry, set up by the Children's Society to investigate what makes a good childhood. They also organise Playday.

Playday 2007 – Our streets too! Street play opinion poll summary

71% of adults report to have played in the street or area near their home everyday when they were a child. This compares to only 21% of children today.

29% of children and young people and 39% of adults said that more space to play would make children and young people play in the streets or area near their home more often. Less danger from traffic was the second most popular solution given by adults (23 per cent), and children put less traffic in their top three solutions.

Traffic is considered the main barrier to neighbourhood play. Nearly 1 in 4 children and young people report that it stops them from playing out on the streets or areas close to their homes.

Adults also consider traffic the main barrier to neighbourhood play. 35% suggest traffic, 32% stranger danger/paedophiles and 22% parents/carers fears prevent children form playing there.

51% of children and young people have at some point been told to stop playing in the streets or area near their homes.

1 in 4 adults reported to have told a child other than their own to stop playing in the street or area near their home. Of these, 39% feared damage to property, compared to 19% who were afraid for the safety of the child or young person.

Only 4% of adults think that children and young people should not be allowed to play/spend time in the streets and area near their home. But 56% of adults think children should be at least 10 years old before they are allowed to play and spend time in the streets and other public areas close to their home.

The street on which they live is very important for children and young people's play,

51% of 7-12 year-old children are not allowed to play out further than their street with out an adult being there.

As children get older they are allowed to play and spend time further away from their home unsupervised by adults. For example, the majority of 15-16 year-olds can play as far as they want, whilst the majority of 13-14 year-olds can play as far as their village/town/district and most 7-8 year-olds can play no further than their street.

56% of adults said that local authorities should take primary responsibility for improving the streets and public areas near their home for children and young people to play and spend time in.

After parks, the street is the second most common place to play when not in the home. 15% of children and young people play most often in the street, topped only by parks, at 26%.

An ICM survey commissioned by Play England for the Playday 2007 Our streets too! campaign. ICM interviewed a random sample of 1030 children and young people aged 7 -16 and 1031 adults across the UK by telephone between 25 June-8 July 2007.

Playing Out
Activities

What, Me Worry?

Before Reading

Reading the Opening

1. A first reading

- Listen to your teacher read the first sentence of this text. As a class make some predictions about the text, for example whether it is fact or fiction, funny or serious and so on, and what you think might happen next.

- Now listen to your teacher read the beginning of this text (below). Again, make some predictions about the rest of the text.

> The only time I have ever broken a bone was also the first time I noticed that adults are not entirely to be counted on. I was four years old and playing on Arthur Bergen's jungle gym when I fell off and broke my leg.
>
> Arthur Bergen lived up the street, but was at the dentist or something when I called, so I decided to have a twirl on his new jungle gym before heading back home.
>
> I don't remember anything at all about the fall, but I do remember very clearly lying on damp earth, the jungle gym now above and around me and seeming awfully large and menacing all of a sudden, and not being able to move my right leg. I remember also lifting my head and looking down my body to my leg which was bent at an unusual – indeed, an entirely novel – angle. I began to call steadily for help, in a variety of tones, but no one heard. Eventually I gave up and dozed a little.

2. A second reading

■ Now re-read the opening together as a class.

■ On your own, take a minute to think about anything you have noticed about the way the text is written so far.

■ Turn to your partner and share your ideas.

■ Share your responses as a whole class.

3. A third reading

■ Re-read the opening once more to yourself. Try to answer the questions that follow.

– What can you tell about the narrator?

– What do you notice about the length of the sentences?

■ With a partner look more closely at three of these words or phrases and the way they have been used in the text. What can you say about why Bryson chose this particular word or phrase?

– Twirl

– Damp earth

– Steadily

– Variety of tones

– Menacing

– Novel

– Not entirely to be counted on.

■ Share your ideas as a class.

———— After Reading ————

Different Responses

1. Your personal response

The title of the chapter is 'What, Me Worry?'.

■ So, did you feel worried about what would happen to the boy?

■ Write a few notes about your personal response, before you discuss the text with anyone else.

2. Two readings

■ Work with a partner. Decide which of you of you will be 'Reader 1' and which of you will be 'Reader 2'.

■ Now look at what the readers have to say about the text in the boxed statements.

– If you are taking the role of Reader 1, think about what might make you become more tense about the boy as you read on. Find as much evidence as you can in the text to support this reading.

– If you are taking the role of Reader 2, think about what might make you become less tense about the boy as you read on. Find as much evidence as you can in the text to support this reading.

Reader 1

'As I read more and more of the text, I started to feel more and more tense about this little boy and what would happen about his broken leg.'

Reader 2

'As I read more and more of the text, I felt less and less tense about this little boy and what would happen about his broken leg.'

■ Now, in role, explain your reading to your partner.

■ Discuss as a class which reading was closest to your personal responses to the text.

A Perfect Afternoon

——— Before Reading ———

Telling a Story

■ In a pair, decide who is A and who is B.

■ A's tell B's a story using these words.

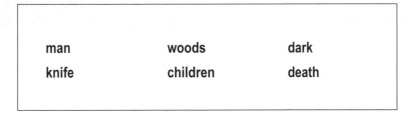

man	woods	dark
knife	children	death

■ Now B's tell A's a story using these words.

■ With your partner discuss the questions that follow.

– Did A's find a story suggested itself to them very quickly or was it difficult to think of a story? Why was this?

– Did B's find it difficult or easy to think of a different story to tell? Why was this?

■ Share your thoughts as a class, feeding back about similarities and differences in the kinds of stories that you told.

——— During Reading ———

Places to 'pause' during reading are marked with a pause button symbol like this:

II

'...the road beyond'

■ Read as far as '...the road beyond'. **II**

■ Discuss with a partner whether you think this story is going to have a happy ending. Why or why not? Look for clues in the text.

■ Now read on, stopping at each of the pause points listed below (**||**) to discuss with your partner whether or not the text will have a happy ending. Look for clues as before:

- Read as far as '…rotting leaves.'
- Read as far as '…chilly and cut off from home.'
- Read as far as '…He said hello'
- Read as far as 'A game of life and death'
- Read as far as 'I nodded.'

■ Now read to the end.

———————— After Reading ————————

A Happy Ending?

■ Now you have read the whole story discuss the questions that follow.

- Do you think the ending is a happy one?
- Why do you think the writer chose the title 'A Perfect Afternoon'?

Assumptions

An assumption is something that is believed to be true without any proof.

■ As a class, remind yourself of the work you did in the starter activity. You probably found that the words you were given led you to make some assumptions, for example that the woods are a dangerous place for children on their own.

The story 'A Perfect Afternoon' plays on some assumptions people make, such as:

- Boys are braver than girls.
- Boys know better than girls.
- Younger children have to do what older children tell them.
- The woods are a dangerous place for children to play on their own.
- A single man in the woods is likely to be dangerous for children.
- Adults know best.
- Adults are the people to go when you have been scared by something.

At the beginning of the story the writer seems to share some of these assumptions but each one is gradually turned around.

What happens to the assumptions in the story?

■ Choose two of the assumptions and write a sentence or two about each one, explaining where in the story the writer seems to share the assumption, and where the assumption is turned around. For example:

People often assume that boys are braver than girls, and at the beginning of the story Peter seems to believe this, calling the girl a 'cry baby'. However, at the end of the story the girl stays to face the man, whereas the boys run away and this shows that she can be just as brave as them, if not more so.

——————— Your Own Writing ———————

A Story from Memory

■ Take yourself back to an early childhood memory. Remember each of the following:

- something you see (for example, the school playground on your first morning in Reception)

- something you hear (for example, the sound of the whistle being blown and the children all falling silent)

- something you smell or taste (for example, the sharp smell of disinfectant in the corridors)

- something you touch or feel (for example, your legs sticking to the plastic chair).

■ Put an imaginary character into your childhood memory, someone quite different from you. What would they make of the situation? How would they respond?

■ Make some notes about your ideas.

■ Start to write a story based on this memory, but from the point of view of the character you imagined.

Be a 'Bad' Parent and Let Your Children Out

Before Reading

Quick Read

■ Read the headline, the first paragraph and the last paragraph, reprinted below.

Headline

> BE A 'BAD' PARENT AND LET YOUR CHILDREN OUT

First paragraph

> I asked my mother yesterday how much freedom she had as a child. 'Well,' she replied, 'I walked to my nursery school in Cambridge alone, aged three, and by four I was roaming the fields behind my house on my hobby-horse.'

Last paragraph

> So let your children out: they are less likely to harm themselves bicycling to the swings than they are bouncing up and down in their own back yard.

■ What can you tell about: the topic, purpose, audience and genre of this text? How do you know?

■ Now read the whole text. Take a minute by yourself to decide what you think about the points the writer is trying to make and whether you agree with her. Make a very short note about your personal response.

——— After Reading ———

Looking at Structure

You are now going to do four activities that will help you to look more closely at how the article is structured and to follow how the writer develops her argument. You will work in pairs and you will need a photocopy of the article.

1. Colour coding

- ■ Choose four different colour highlighters (or decide on four different ways to underline the text). Look for the four aspects of the text given below and, when you find them, colour code (or underline) them in the article.

    - Alice Thomson's memories of her childhood

    - Her mother's memories of her own childhood

    - Facts and statistics

    - Her own behaviour as a parent

- ■ What do you notice?

- ■ Why do you think she structures the article in this way? What effect might this have on the reader? For example, why do you think she doesn't give any facts and statistics until half way through the article?

2. Yes, and... Yes, but...

- ■ Re-read the text as far as '…he didn't trouble us.'

- ■ Annotate the text with as many 'yes, but…' or 'yes, and…' comments as you can. 'Yes, but…' comments show that there is a part of the text you disagree with, or that you think has not been argued very well. 'Yes, and…' comments show that there is part of the text that you agree with, or where you could take the ideas further. For example, after the sentence '…by four I was roaming the fields behind my house on my hobby horse' you might comment:

    Yes, but things were safer for children in those days.

or

    Yes, and isn't it a shame that young children no longer have that freedom.

■ Re-read the second half of the article. As you read:

- continue to annotate the text with 'yes, but…' or 'yes, and…' comments

- notice whether the writer answers any of your 'yes, buts' from the first half of the article.

- notice whether anything she writes support any of your 'yes, ands' from the first part of the article.

3. Using facts and statistics

■ Look at the Survey on page 22.

■ Which facts and statistics from the survey has Alice Thomson used in her article?

■ Which other facts and statistics could she have used from the survey to support her argument? What facts and statistics has she used from another source?

■ Do you think the facts and statistics she has chosen support her argument and help to persuade the reader?

4. Discussing the structure

■ As a class, think about what you have discovered through doing the activities and then discuss the questions that follow.

- How does Alice Thomson try to persuade you to her point of view?

- How does she use facts and statistics in the article?

- How does she structure her argument?

- Is she successful in persuading you that parents should give their children more freedom?

Children 'Scared' to Play Outside

—————————— Before Reading ——————————

Do You Watch *Newsround*?

■ Turn to your partner and tell them whether you watch *Newsround* and why or why not.

■ As a class, discuss what you know about the *Newsround* audience, including a discussion of the questions that follow.

– What is the age range of children who watch the programme?

– Why do people watch it?

– What do those of you who have seen the programme like or dislike about it?

—————————— During Reading ——————————

Who, What, Where, When, Why?

New journalists are told they must make sure that any news story tells the audience:

– Who are the people involved?

– What happened?

– Where did it happen?

– When did it happen?

– Why did it happen?

■ As you read the story, notice whether it answers each of these questions.

After Reading

The Audience

■ In pairs, discuss how suitable you think the article is for the *Newsround* audience of 7-14 year-olds. Use the questions below to start your discussion.

– Is this a story the audience would be interested in? Why or why not?

– Is the story written in a way that is easy to understand, but still reports the facts? Why or why not?

– Is the story written in a way that would interest the *Newsround* audience? Why or why not?

■ As a class, discuss any improvements you would make to the story to make it interesting and easy to understand for the *Newsround* audience.

Choosing Images

■ Imagine you are *Newsround* editors. You have several pieces of film footage and you must choose three of them to show while the story is being read. In a group of three or four, look at the different choices below and decide which pieces of film you would use to illustrate different sections of the story. Keep the work you did on audience in mind. When you have made your decisions, explain your choices to the class.

– An old, neglected playground.

– Children hanging round some flats, looking bored.

– A boy playing a computer game.

– An overweight girl watching television.

– Some children playing football, unsupervised.

– Some children at a football coaching session.

– A boy riding off on his bike.

– A notice on a wall saying 'No ball games.'

– A girl climbing a tree.

– Two children in the back of a car, in a traffic jam.

– The Children's Society spokeswoman talking to an interviewer.

– Film of children playing at an event from last year's Playday, with the Playday logo in the background.

Playday

———— Before Reading ————

Group Memory Game

■ Your teacher will put a photocopy of a leaflet for an organisation called 'Playday' on a table outside the classroom. You are going to work together in groups of three or four to reproduce as much of the leaflet as you can on a piece of A3 or sugar paper. You are not expected to reproduce all of it, just see how much you can do. Read all the instructions below before you start as this will help your group to think of good strategies for working together.

  – You have three minutes to discuss as a group what strategies you will use to collect the information.

  – Each of you will then spend up to one minute looking at the leaflet outside the room.

  – When you have finished looking, you should return to your group and spend three minutes working with your group on the leaflet before the next person goes to look.

  – Each of you can look at the leaflet twice.

■ When you have finished the game, walk round the class looking at what other groups managed to do, noticing similarities and differences in which sections of the leaflet people were able to reproduce.

———— After Reading ————

Reflecting on the Group Memory Game

■ Which bits of the leaflet were the easiest or hardest to remember? Why? You should think about elements of the text such as content, layout, photographs, font size and type, bullet points, logo and so on.

■ What can you now say about the layout of the leaflet?

■ How do you think the leaflet could be improved to make it more eye-catching and more appealing to read?

Your Playday Event

In this activity you will be working in role as youth consultants to a local group organizing a Playday event for young people in your area. The local group is made up of parents, youth workers, representatives from the local council and local volunteers.

■ You are going to advise the local group on a Playday event which would appeal to young people in your area. Your activity should fit with the theme 'Give us a go' and the 'Important messages' listed in the Playday leaflet.

1. Coming up with an idea

■ Working in groups of four, allocate roles in your group. You will need: a chairperson; a recorder; a creative thinker; a real world thinker.

- The chairperson keeps the group on track and makes sure everyone contributes.

- The recorder takes note of your ideas.

- The creative thinker is responsible for thinking of as many ideas as they can, without worrying about whether they would really be possible.

- The real world thinker is responsible for thinking about how things would work in practice.

If you will be working on this project for more than one lesson, you should rotate these roles.

■ Re-read the 'important messages' listed in the leaflet and discuss what they mean. Check the meaning of any words and phrases you don't understand.

■ Spend around ten minutes brainstorming ideas for your event. Your chairperson is responsible for making sure you keep to the ground rules that follow.

- Don't reject or comment on ideas at this stage.

- Brainstorm at least fifteen event ideas. When you keep brainstorming like this you can sometimes come up with a surprising and unexpected idea.

■ Now spend around twenty minutes discussing the ideas you have had and exploring the possible problems with putting some of the ideas into practice. Narrow your choices down to four strong ideas. Help your group to be creative by using the following suggestions:

– Be positive. Don't put people's ideas down.

– Use phrases like the ones below to explore your ideas.

– I wonder if...?

– What would happen if…?

– Would it work if…?

– What about…?

– How could we solve the problem of…?

2. Testing your ideas

■ Each person in your group is going to take fifteen minutes to prepare a short presentation on one of your four ideas. In your presentation you should explain:

– why this event would appeal to young people your age

– how the event fits with the 'important messages' of the Playday campaign

– what problems there might be with putting this idea into practice, and how you would solve them.

■ Make your presentation to the group.

3. Make a final decision

■ Based on the presentations, take around fifteen minutes to make a final decision about which event you will present to the local group.

4. Presenting to the local group

■ As a class, listen to the presentations on the chosen ideas from each group of consultants.

■ In role as members of the local group, discuss and choose the idea you think would work best.

━━━━━━━━━━ **Your Own Writing** ━━━━━━━━━━

A Leaflet for Your Event

You are going to create a leaflet to get people to come along to your event.

- ■ As a class, remind yourselves of the activity you did on the layout of the Playday leaflet. What helped to make the leaflet memorable and eye catching? What could have been improved?

- ■ Make a rough draft of some ideas for your leaflet. Use the Survey on page 22 to help you to include some facts and statistics.

- ■ Write up your final idea as a brief for the Creative Department who will develop your leaflet. In your writing, include:

  - a rough draft of your design

  - an explanation of what will make the design eye catching and appealing

  - an explanation of how your leaflet will put across the important messages

  - why you think your leaflet will appeal to young people your age.

Working with More than One Text

Be a 'Bad' Parent and Children 'Scared' to Play Outside

- ■ You are going to turn 'Be a 'Bad' Parent' into a story for *Newsround*. Begin by reminding yourself of your work on the audience for the report on the *Newsround* website.

- ■ Now re-read the article 'Be a 'Bad' Parent'. With a partner discuss what you think the problems will be in turning the story into something suitable for *Newsround*. You could use the prompts below to get you started.

  The 'Be a 'Bad' Parent' article is written in the first person ('I') whereas the Newsround story is written in the third person ('s/he')

- ■ Make a class list of the problems you came up with.

- ■ With your partner, discuss how you could solve some of the problems.

- ■ Share your thoughts as a class.

- ■ Write the first line of the *Newsround* story together as a class.

- ■ Write the rest of the story for by yourself. When you have finished, read it to check that you have answered the questions who, what, when, where, why.

- ■ Listen to some of the stories being read aloud and, as a class, discuss some of the ways different people have solved the writing problems.

It's a Dog's Life

Bat Loves the Night

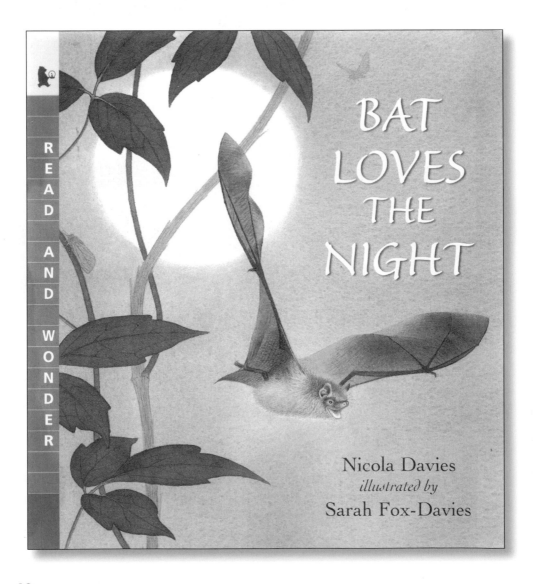

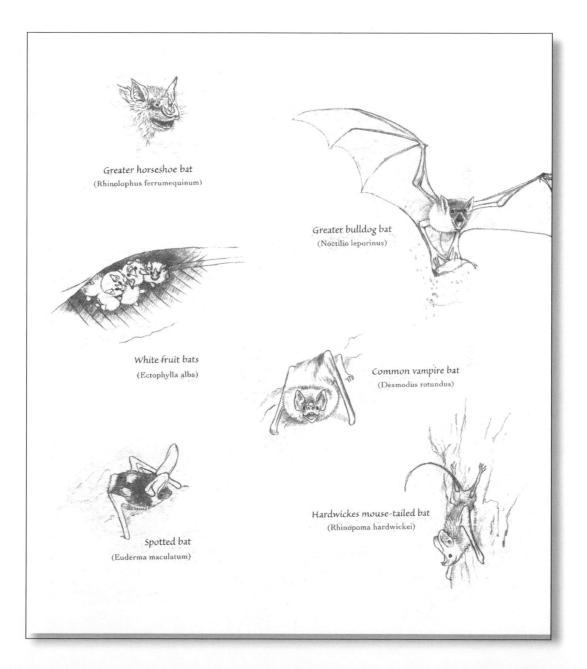

Greater horseshoe bat
(Rhinolophus ferrumequinum)

Greater bulldog bat
(Noctilio leporinus)

White fruit bats
(Ectophylla alba)

Common vampire bat
(Desmodus rotundus)

Spotted bat
(Euderma maculatum)

Hardwickes mouse-tailed bat
(Rhinopoma hardwickei)

Bats are the only mammals that can really fly,
and flight has made them very successful.
There are more than nine hundred species, living in
almost every habitat from subarctic tundra to
tropical forests and deserts. Birds may rule the air
by day, but bats are the monarchs of the night.

This book is about one of the pipistrelle bats.
Pipistrelles are found around the world,
from North America to Africa, Europe,
Asia and Australia.

Bat is waking,
upside down as usual,
hanging by her toenails.

Her beady eyes open.
Her pixie ears twitch.

She shakes her
thistledown fur.

6

43

She unfurls her wings,
made of skin so fine the finger bones
inside show through.

*This pipistrelle bat
is no bigger than
your thumb.*

*A bat's wing is its
arm and hand.
Four extra-long fingers
support the skin of the wing.*

7

44

Bats' toes are shaped like hooks,
so it's no effort for a bat to hang
upside down.

Now she unhooks her toes
and drops into black space.
With a sound like a tiny umbrella
opening, she flaps her wings.

Bat is flying.

8

Out!

Out under the broken tile
into the night-time garden.

11

Over bushes, under trees,
between fence posts,
through the tangled hedge
she swoops untouched.
Bat is at home in the darkness,
as a fish is in the water.
She doesn't need to see –
she can hear where she is going.

*Bats can see. But in the dark, good ears
are more useful than eyes.*

12

Bat shouts as she flies, louder than
a hammer blow, higher than a squeak.
She beams her voice around her like a
torch, and the echoes come singing back.
They carry a sound-picture of all
her voice has touched.
Listening hard, Bat can hear every
detail, the smallest twigs, the
shape of leaves.

Using sound to find your way like this
is called echolocation.
    Some bats shout through their mouth,
    and some shout through their nose.

14

Nicola Davies, illus. Sarah Fox-Davies:
Bat Loves the Night (2001)

The Emissary

Martin knew it was autumn again, for Dog ran into the house bringing wind and frost and a smell of apples turned to cider under trees. In dark clocksprings of hair, Dog fetched goldenrod, dust of farewell summer, acorn-husk, hair of squirrel, feather of departed robin, sawdust from fresh-cut cordwood, and leaves like charcoals shaken from a blaze of maple trees. Dog jumped. Showers of brittle fern, blackberry vine, marsh-grass sprang over the bed where Martin shouted. No doubt, no doubt of it at all, this incredible beast was October!

'Here, boy, here!'

And Dog settled to warm Martin's body with all the bonfires and subtle burnings of the season, to fill the room with soft or heavy, wet or dry odours of far-travelling. In spring, he smelled of lilac, iris, lawn-mowered grass; in summer, ice-cream-moustached, he came pungent with firecracker, Roman candle, pinwheel, baked by the sun. But autumn! Autumn!

'Dog, what's it like outside?'

And lying there, Dog told as he always told. Lying there, Martin found autumn as in the old days before sickness bleached him white on his bed. Here was his contact, his carry-all, the quick-moving part of himself he sent with a yell to run and return, circle and scent, collect and deliver the time and texture of worlds in town, country, by creek, river, lake, down-cellar, up-attic, in closet or coal-bin. Ten dozen times a day he was gifted with sunflower seed, cinder-path, milkweed, horse-chestnut, or full flame-smell of pumpkin. Through the loomings of the universe Dog shuttled; the design was hid in his pelt. Put out your hand, it was there...

'And where did you go this morning?'

But he knew without hearing where Dog had rattled down hills where autumn lay in cereal crispness, where children lay in funeral pyres, in rustling heaps, the leaf buried but watchful dead, as Dog and the world blew by. Martin trembled his fingers, searched the thick fur, read the long journey. Through stubbled fields, over glitters of ravine creek, down marbled spread of cemetery yard, into woods. In the great season of spices and rare incense, now Martin ran through his emissary, around, about, and home!

The bedroom door opened.

'That dog of yours is in trouble again.'

Mother brought in a tray of fruit salad, cocoa, and toast, her blue eyes snapping.

'Mother...'

'Always digging places. Dug a hole in Miss Tarkin's garden this morning. She's spittin' mad. That's the fourth hole he's dug there this week.'

'Maybe he's looking for something.'

'Fiddlesticks, he's too darned curious. If he doesn't behave he'll be locked up.'

Martin looked at this woman as if she were a stranger.

'Oh, you wouldn't do that! How would I learn anything? How would I find things out if Dog didn't tell me?'

Mom's voice was quieter. 'Is that what he does – tell you things?'

'There's nothing I don't know when he goes out and around and back, *nothing* I can't find out from him!'

They both sat looking at Dog and the dry strewings of mould and seed over the quilt.

'Well, if he'll just stop digging where he shouldn't, he can run all he wants,' said Mother.

'Here, boy, here!'

And Martin snapped a tin note to the dog's collar:

> MY OWNER IS MARTIN SMITH – TEN YEARS OLD –
>
> SICK IN BED – VISITORS WELCOME.

Dog barked. Mother opened the downstairs door and let him out.

Martin sat listening.

Far off and away you could hear Dog in the quiet autumn rain that was falling now. You could hear the barking-jingling fade, rise, fade again as he cut down alley, over lawn, to fetch back Mr Holloway and the oiled metallic smell of the delicate snowflake-interiored watches he repaired in his home shop. Or maybe he would bring Mr Jacobs, the grocer, whose clothes were rich with lettuce, celery, tomatoes, and the secret tinned and hidden smell of red demons stamped on cans of devilled ham. Mr Jacobs and his unseen pink-meat devils waved often from the yard below. Or Dog brought Mr Jackson, Mrs Gillespie, Mr Smith, Mrs Holmes, *any* friend or near-friend, encountered, cornered, begged, worried, and at last shepherded home for lunch, or tea-and-biscuits.

Now, listening, Martin heard Dog below, with footsteps moving in a light rain behind him. The downstairs bell rang. Mom opened the door, light voices murmured. Martin sat forward, face shining. The stair treads creaked. A young woman's voice laughed quietly. Miss Haight, of course, his teacher from school!

The bedroom door sprang open.

Martin had company.

Morning, afternoon, evening, dawn and dusk, sun and moon circled with Dog, who faithfully reported temperatures of turf and air, colour of earth and tree, consistency of mist or rain, but – most important of all – brought back again and again – Miss Haight.

On Saturday, Sunday and Monday she baked Martin orange-iced cupcakes, brought him library books about dinosaurs and cavemen. On Tuesday, Wednesday and Thursday somehow he beat her at dominoes, somehow she lost at checkers, and soon, she cried, he'd defeat her handsomely at chess. On Friday, Saturday and Sunday they talked and never stopped talking, and she was so young and laughing and handsome and her hair was a soft, shining brown like the season outside the window, and she walked clear, clean and quick, a heartbeat warm in the bitter afternoon when he heard it. Above all, she had the secret of signs, and could read and interpret Dog and the symbols she searched out and plucked forth from his coat with her miraculous fingers. Eyes shut, softly laughing, in a gypsy's voice, she divined the world from the treasures in her hands.

And on Monday afternoon, Miss Haight was dead.

Martin sat up in bed, slowly.

'Dead?' he whispered.

Dead, said his mother, yes, dead, killed in an auto accident a mile out of town. Dead, yes, dead, which meant cold to Martin, which meant silence and whiteness and winter come long before its time. Dead, silent, cold, white. The thoughts circled round, blew down, and settled in whispers.

Martin held Dog, thinking; turned to the wall. The lady with the autumn-coloured hair. The lady with the laughter that was very gentle and never made fun and the eyes that watched your mouth to see everything you ever said. The-other-half-of-autumn-lady, who told what was left untold by Dog, about the world. The heartbeat at the still centre of grey afternoon. The heartbeat fading...

'Mom? What do they do in the graveyard, Mom, under the ground? Just lay there?'

'*Lie* there.'

'Lie there? Is that *all* they do? It doesn't sound like much fun.'

'For goodness' sake, it's not made out to be fun.'

'Why don't they jump up and run around once in a while if they get tired lying there? God's pretty silly –'

'Martin!'

'Well, you'd think He'd treat people better than to tell them to lie still for keeps. That's impossible. Nobody can do it! I tried once. Dog tries. I tell him, 'dead Dog!' He plays dead awhile, then gets sick and tired and wags his tail or opens one eye and looks at me, bored. Boy, I bet sometimes those graveyard people do the same, huh, Dog?'

Dog barked.

'Be still with that kind of talk!' said Mother.

Martin looked off into space.

'Bet that's exactly what they do,' he said.

Autumn burnt the trees bare and ran Dog still farther around, fording creek, prowling graveyard as was his custom, and back in the dusk to fire off volleys of barking that shook windows wherever he turned.

In the late last days of October, Dog began to act as if the wind had changed and blew from a strange country. He stood quivering on the porch below. He whined, his eyes fixed at the empty land beyond town. He brought no visitors for Martin. He stood for hours each day, as if leashed, trembling, then shot away straight, as if someone had called. Each night, he returned later, with no one following. Each night, Martin sank deeper and deeper in his pillow.

'Well, people are busy,' said Mother. 'They haven't time to notice the tag Dog carries. Or they mean to come visit, but forget.'

But there was more to it than that. There was the fevered shining in Dog's eyes, and his whimpering tic late at night, in some private dream. His shivering in the dark, under the bed. The way he sometimes stood half the night, looking at Martin as if some great and impossible secret was his and he knew no way to tell it save by savagely thumping his tail, or turning in endless circles, never to lie down, spinning and spinning again.

On October thirtieth, Dog ran out and didn't come back at all, even when after supper Martin heard his parents call and call. The hour grew late, the streets and sidewalks stood empty, the air moved cold about the house and there was nothing, nothing.

Long after midnight, Martin lay watching the world beyond the cool, clear glass windows. Now there was not even autumn, for there was no Dog to fetch it in. There would be no winter, for who could bring the snow to melt in your hands? Father, Mother? No, not the same. They couldn't play the game with its special secrets and rules, its sounds and pantomimes. No more seasons. No more time. The go-between, the emissary, was lost to the wild throngings of civilization, poisoned, stolen, hit by a car, left somewhere in a culvert...

Sobbing, Martin turned his face to his pillow. The world was a picture under glass, untouchable. The world was dead.

Martin twisted in bed and in three days the last Hallowe'en pumpkins were rotting in trash cans, papier-mâché skulls and witches were burnt on bonfires, and ghosts were stacked on shelves with other linens until next year.

To Martin, Hallowe'en had been nothing more than one evening when tin horns cried off in the cold autumn stars, children blew like goblin leaves along the flinty walks, flinging their heads, or cabbages, at porches, soap-writing names or similar magic symbols on icy windows. All of it as distant, unfathomable, and nightmarish as a puppet show seen from so many miles away that there is no sound or meaning.

For three days in November, Martin watched alternate light and shadow sift across his ceiling. The fire-pageant was over forever; autumn lay in cold ashes. Martin sank deeper, yet deeper in white marble layers of bed, motionless, listening always listening...

Friday evening, his parents kissed him good night and walked out of the house into the hushed cathedral weather towards a motion-picture show. Miss Tarkin from next door stayed on in the parlour below until Martin called down he was sleepy, then took her knitting off home.

In silence, Martin lay following the great move of stars down a clear and moonlit sky, remembering nights such as this when he'd spanned the town with Dog ahead, behind, around about, tracking the green-plush ravine, lapping slumbrous streams gone milky with the fullness of the moon, leaping cemetery tombstones while whispering the marble names; on, quickly on, through shaved meadows where the only motion was the off-on quivering of stars, to streets where shadows would not stand aside for you but crowded all the sidewalks for mile on mile. Run now run! Chasing, being chased by bitter smoke, fog, mist, wind, ghost of mind, fright of memory; home, safe, sound, snug-warm, asleep...

Nine o'clock.

Chime. The drowsy clock in the deep stairwell below. Chime.

Dog, come home, and run the world with you. Dog, bring a thistle with frost on it, or bring nothing else but the wind. Dog, where *are* you? Oh, listen, now, I'll call.

Martin held his breath.

Way off somewhere – a sound.

Martin rose up, trembling.

There, again – the sound.

So small a sound, like a sharp needle-point brushing the sky long miles and many miles away.

The dreamy echo of a dog – barking.

The sound of a dog crossing fields and farms, dirt roads and rabbit paths, running, running, letting out great barks of steam, cracking the night. The sound of a circling dog which came and went, lifted and faded, opened up, shut in, moved forward, went back, as if the animal were kept by someone on a fantastically long chain. As if the dog were running and someone whistled under the chestnut trees, in mould-shadow, tar-shadow, moon-shadow, walking, and the dog circled back and sprang out again towards home.

Dog! Martin thought, oh Dog, come home, boy! Listen, oh, listen, where you *been*? Come on, boy, make tracks!

Five, ten, fifteen minutes; near, very near, the bark, the sound. Martin cried out, thrust his feet from the bed, leaned to the window. Dog! Listen, boy! Dog! Dog! He said it over and over. Dog! Dog! Wicked Dog, run off and gone all these days! Bad Dog, good Dog, home, boy, hurry, and bring what you can!

Near now, near, up the street, barking, to knock clapboard housefronts with sound, whirl iron cocks on rooftops in the moon, firing off volleys – Dog! now at the door below...

Martin shivered.

Should he run – let Dog in, or wait for Mom and Dad? Wait? Oh, God, wait? But what if Dog ran off again? No, he'd go down, snatch the door wide, yell, grab Dog in, and run upstairs so fast, laughing, crying, holding tight, that...

Dog stopped barking.

Hey! Martin almost broke the window, jerking to it.

Silence. As if someone had told Dog to hush now, hush, hush.

A full minute passed. Martin clenched his fists.

Below, a faint whimpering.

Then, slowly, the downstairs front door opened. Someone was kind enough to have opened the door for Dog. Of course! Dog had brought Mr Jacobs or Mr Gillespie or Miss Tarkin, or …

The downstairs door shut.

Dog raced upstairs, whining, flung himself on the bed.

'Dog, Dog, where've you *been*, what've you *done*! Dog, Dog!'

And he crushed Dog hard and long to himself, weeping. Dog, Dog. He laughed and shouted. Dog! But after a moment he stopped laughing and crying, suddenly.

He pulled away. He held the animal and looked at him, eyes widening.

The odour coming from Dog was different.

It was a smell of strange earth. It was a smell of night within night, the smell of digging down deep in shadow through earth that had lain cheek by jowl with things that were long hidden and decayed. A stinking and rancid soil fell away in clods of dissolution from Dog's muzzle and paws. He had dug deep. He had dug very deep indeed. That *was* it, wasn't it? wasn't it? *wasn't* it!

What kind of message was this from Dog? What could such a message mean? The stench – the ripe and awful cemetery earth.

Dog was a bad dog, digging where he shouldn't. Dog was a good dog, always making friends. Dog loved people. Dog brought them home.

And now, moving up the dark hall stairs, at intervals, came the sound of feet, one foot dragged after the other, painfully, slowly, slowly, slowly.

Dog shivered. A rain of strange night earth fell seething on the bed.

Dog turned.

The bedroom door whispered in.

Martin had company.

Ray Bradbury: Ghost Stories (ed Robert Westall, 2004)

Siren Screams

This text consists of a question and two replies from the 'Last Word' column of New Scientist magazine. Readers write in with a science or technology question and other readers write in with their answers.

When emergency sirens pass by, all the dogs in my neighbourhood yowl. The reason, I've read, is that the sound of the siren hurts their sensitive ears. Yet my cat, whose hearing seems to be more sensitive than my dog's, pays no attention. Why would the sound hurt a dog's ears and not those of a cat?

Michael Ham, Monterey, California, US

The reason dogs yowl when emergency services go by may be because, to the dogs, the siren sounds like other dogs howling and they respond by howling back. This goes back to the time when they hunted in packs and signalled to one another when searching for prey. Even if the siren does not mimic exactly the sound of another dog, they can probably pick out a component part of the screaming siren that does. Cats, on the other hand, hunt alone, are not pack animals and so do not respond to the sirens.

Anne Bloomberg, London, UK

Your correspondent might like to read the excellent *Dogwatching: Why dogs bark and other canine mysteries explained*. In it, anthropologist Desmond Morris answers 46 FAQs. He mentions that families who attempt to sing music together are sometimes helped, or hindered, by their dog, which joins in when its human family breaks into a group howl.

Dogs, wolves and humans evolved as cooperative hunters, and more recently, sheep guardians, with a need to keep in touch with their partners on the next ridge. Hence howling, yodelling and such devices as the Israeli *challil*, or shepherd's flute. Sirens are artificial, amplified howling. Their rise and fall is calculated to alarm and stir us and to my ear, and my dogs' ears, they succeed splendidly.

Ann Bradford Drummond, Micanopy, Florida, US

New Scientist: Does Anything Eat Wasps and 101 Other Questions (2005)

Who Let the Dogs Out?

It was Red the lurcher

With the light fading fast, a lone figure slides back the steel bolt, tugs open the cell-like door and slips out.

Glancing about to avoid the diminished night-time security, he moves quickly towards his destination: the kitchen.

But as anyone who has ever had an illicit midnight feast will know, they are not half as much fun without pals.

Red the lurcher astonished staff at Battersea Dogs' Home in south London by learning not only to unbolt his kennel door, but then to liberate his favourite canine companions to join the fun.

Staff at the animal shelter were baffled when for several mornings in a row they arrived for work to find several dogs had escaped and wreaked havoc in the kitchens.

Determined to find the culprit, managers installed video surveillance on Thursday night.

They saw four year-old Red reaching up on his hind paws and using his nose and teeth to undo the bolt securing the door to his caged accommodation.

Even more astonishing was the sight of him then moving swiftly from kennel to kennel performing the same trick to free other dogs.

Becky Blackmore, of Battersea Dogs' Home, said: 'We had come in to chaos in the morning. It happened probably about a dozen times. We would come in to lots of dogs out on their block.

'They had had lots of food, lots of fun and games and caused loads of mess. We weren't too sure what was going on. There are lots of stories about Battersea being haunted so we wanted to make sure that there was an explanation for what was going on and we managed to catch the culprit.

'It is amazing really because lurchers aren't particularly renowned for their intelligence.'

Staff believed that Red's emaciated state when he was rescued as a stray in June could explain his determination to track down food. They are hoping his new-found fame will help to secure him a new home.

Rescue services believe a cat saved its owner when a fire broke out at her home. Evelyne Holloway, 68, of Kingsclere, Hants, was woken by her 14 year-old cat, Sooty, scratching her.

Nic Fleming: The Telegraph (2006)

Cameras Show Who Let the Dogs Out

R ed 'only ever chooses to let out his mates'.

A dog has been caught on camera breaking out of his kennel at Battersea Dogs Home and freeing other animals for regular midnight feasts.

Red has been unlocking his kennel using his nose and teeth before releasing his favourite canine companions.

Staff at the south London animal shelter decided to install cameras after arriving each day to find food everywhere and dogs running amok.

The lurcher's kennel has now been made more secure to stop him escaping.

Liz Emeny, from the home, told BBC News Online the most dogs Red had ever released in one night was nine.

Red's kennel has now been made more secure

'For the last two weeks staff have been arriving every morning to a complete mess with dogs and food everywhere,' she said.

'He [Red] only ever chooses his mates to let out, with Lucky, the dog who he was found with, being the first to be freed.

'We don't have CCTV cameras in the corridor so couldn't work out how he was doing it so we asked a film company to set up some cameras.'

The three-year-old lurcher has been at the home since June after being handed into a London police station in an emaciated state.

'Lurchers aren't usually known for their intelligence but Red is such an inquisitive dog and would be so easy to train,' Ms Emeny added.

BBC News Online (2006)

It's a Dog's Life
Activities

Bat Loves the Night

Before Reading

What Kind of Text?

■ Read the extract below and then discuss the questions that follow with a partner.

   – What kind of text do you think this is from? What is the audience, purpose and genre?

   – What makes you think this?

Bat is waking, upside down as usual, hanging by her toenails.
Her beady eyes open. Her pixie ears twitch.
She shakes her thistledown fur.

After Reading

Your Response

■ Read the rest of the text on pages 40-48, then discuss the questions below.

   – Have you changed your mind about what type of text this is?

   – What clues have you used to help you think about the genre, purpose and audience?

   – Which features typical of *fiction* do you notice (for example: similes, metaphors, interesting verbs, active voice, varied sentence construction)?

   – Which features typical of *non-fiction* do you notice (for example: facts, terminology, footnotes, no opinions, about people not things)?

   – What can you say about the way the text looks on the page?

Your Own Writing

A Book for Young Children

You are going to produce a short book for young children in the same series as *Bat Loves the Night*.

- ■ As a class, choose an animal to write about. Decide how you are going to write your book by discussing the questions that follow.

  - – Who is your audience (what age group)? What difference will this make to the way you write your text?

  - – Will you write about one individual animal? Or about this kind of animal in general?

  - – What kind of information do you need to include. Look again at the extract from *Bat Loves the Night* to help you to decide.

  - – Which features of *Bat Loves the Night* are you going to use to interest the reader?

A KWL Grid

A KWL grid is a way of organising your research. KWL stands for 'what we **K**now', what we **W**ould like to know' and 'what we've **L**earnt'.

- ■ Draw a grid with three columns on a large piece of sugar paper, like the one below: what we know, what we would like to know, what we've learnt. Fill in the first column as a class by sharing everything you know about the animal you have chosen to write about. Fill in the second column as a series of questions to be answered, thinking about what other kinds of information you need to include, such as the animal's habitat, special features, interesting facts and so on.

What we know	What we would like to know	What we've learnt

- ■ Working in groups, divide the questions amongst the class.

- ■ Put the KWL grid on the wall so that you can fill in answers to the questions as you discover them.

- ■ Research the answer to the questions you have been given. You could use the internet, or ask your school or local library to create a book box.

Beginning to Write

■ As a class, take one of the facts you have found out. Brainstorm some similes and metaphors, adjectives, adverbs and verbs you could use to write about this fact. Write a sentence or two as a class, discussing the choices you make as you write. You should think about:

- how to make your writing suitable for the age group

- how to make your writing interesting

- how to make the facts fascinating.

■ You are now going to write your own book. It should be around 200 words long. If you have time, you could think about how to lay out your writing with illustrations and footnotes.

Extension Work

■ As a bigger project, if you have more time, you could make links with a local primary school. You could then:

- go into a class and interview the children to find out what animals they are interested in and what they like in a non-fiction book

- use what you have found out to help you to produce a first draft of your book.

■ Go back to the class to read them the first draft of the book you have produced and get some feed back to help you to re-draft your book.

The Emissary

─────────── **Before Reading** ───────────

The word 'emissary' comes from two linked Latin words: '*emittere*' which means 'to send out' and '*emissarius*' meaning 'spy'. An emissary is someone who is sent out on a special mission. Their role could be as a messenger or a representative, or to promote the mission or gather information. In the story the word 'emissary' is used for a dog belonging to a boy who has been ill in bed for a long time.

- As a class, brainstorm some ideas about why this dog might be described as an 'emissary'.

─────────── **During Reading** ───────────

Mood Swings 1

- Listen to this piece being read aloud, either by your teacher or by another student.

- Listen out for any changes of mood or atmosphere in the text. For example, the first paragraph sets the autumnal atmosphere. This shifts slightly to show the warm relationship between Dog and Martin when he asks 'Dog, what's it like outside?'. Then the mood changes more sharply at 'The bedroom door opened' as Mother comes in, angry about the trouble Dog has caused.

─────────── **After Reading** ───────────

Personal Response

- Think to yourself for a moment about your response to the story. What did it make you think or feel?

- Now that you have read the story, why do you think it is called 'The Emissary'?

- Share your thoughts with the person sitting next to you.

Shared Response

For this activity you will need to have the statements below photocopied onto separate cards, or have the statements written on post-it notes or pieces of paper.

■ Working in a pair or a small group, write the title of the story, 'The Emissary', in the middle of a piece of paper.

■ Read through the statements below and discuss which ones you agree with. Put any you disagree with to one side.

■ Now read each of the statements you have left again. Discuss which statements seem to best sum up the story.

■ As you discuss the statements, place or stick them on the paper. The better you think a statement sums up the story, the closer you should place it to the title of the story written in the middle of the paper. If there are any statements you just can't agree on, place those to one side and discuss them again at the end.

This is a story about the friendship between a boy and a dog.	**1**	
This is a ghost story.	**2**	
This is a story about death.	**3**	
At the end of the story, Miss Haight comes to visit Martin.	**4**	
This is a sad story.	**5**	
This is a scary story.	**6**	
This is a realistic story.	**7**	

Martin's mother doesn't understand why Dog is so important to Martin.	**8**
The writer leaves us with a mystery at the end of the story, we don't know what has happened.	**9**
The story makes the reader feel very sympathetic to Martin.	**10**
This is a story about loneliness.	**11**

Mood Swings 2

- As a class, discuss the points where you noted changes in mood in the story.

- Imagine that you are preparing a reading of the story for the radio. You would need a soundtrack to go with the reading that highlighted the mood and atmosphere and any places where this seems to change.

- With a partner discuss your first thoughts about what kind of music you might use and whether you would use any other sound effects.

- On your own, choose a section of the story about two pages long. Working on a photocopy of the text, note what sounds you would use and where they would change. Note any changes you would make in the volume as well as the type of music or sound effect. Compare and discuss your notes with at least one other person.

- If there is time, you could create your soundtrack and play it to the class as you read the piece.

——— Your Own Writing ———

As Martin is confined to bed, he cannot look outside to see autumn, he can only experience it through the things Dog brings home.

- Read the opening again, as far as 'Dog, what's it like outside?'. Notice the things Bradbury describes to help both Martin and the reader to imagine autumn.

- Imagine Dog coming home to Martin in a different season. What clues would he bring with him? If you have time, research what plants and birds are typical of the season you are going to describe.

- Write between two and five paragraphs in the style of 'The Emissary', describing Dog coming into Martin's room and bringing clues with him about the season and the weather.

Siren Screams

On the last page of the *New Scientist* magazine is a column called 'Last Word'. For this column, readers write in with a science or technology question and then other readers write in with their answers. The best answers are published and, as this is *New Scientist* magazine, many of the people who write in are experts. However, the experts don't always agree and so there are often several different possible answers to a question.

Before Reading

Fact and Opinion

- A **fact** is something that can be proven, that can be shown to exist, or shown to be true.

- An **opinion** is someone's view or judgement about something, or a conclusion they have drawn from looking at the evidence.

- An **assertion** is when someone states strongly that something is true, even though they don't have any evidence to back up what they are saying.

■ Read the statements below and decide which you think are fact, which are opinion and which are assertion. Share your ideas as a class, including the reasons for your decisions.

– The reason people have eyebrows is to keep sweat and rain out of their eyes.

– Fresh fruit is tasty.

– Having plants in a room makes me feel more peaceful.

– Fresh fruit is good for you.

– Research shows that having plants in a room makes people feel more peaceful.

– The Earth orbits the sun.

– The Earth will always orbit the sun.

– The reason people have eyebrows may be to keep sweat and rain out of their eyes.

■ As a class discuss which statements you found it easy to categorise as fact, opinion or assertion, and which ones it was difficult to decide about. Why was this?

Howling Dogs

A reader wrote to the *New Scientist* magazine with the following question:

> *W*hen emergency sirens pass by, all the dogs in my neighbourhood yowl. The reason, I've read, is that the sound of the siren hurts their sensitive ears. Yet my cat, whose hearing seems to be more sensitive than my dog's, pays no attention. Why would the sound hurt a dog's ears and not those of a cat?

■ Write a short reply to this person (off the top of your head, without research) suggesting an answer to his question.

———————— After Reading ————————

Convincing Replies

■ Which reply is the most convincing: yours, Anne Bloomberg's or Ann Bradford's?

■ With a partner discuss what makes an answer convincing. Think about the aspects suggested below to get your discussion started.

- How many facts are included and what effect this has on the reader.

- How many assertions are included and what effect this has on the reader.

- How many opinions are included and what effect this has on the reader.

- The kind of vocabulary that is used. Choose two or three particular words and phrases which made the reply convincing.

- The length of the sentences and what effect this has on the reader.

- Whether the sentences are simple or complex and what effect this has on the reader.

Your Own Writing

A Convincing Reply

■ You are now going to take another question from *Does Anything Eat Wasps?*. With a partner you are going to use the facts below to write an answer. Use what you have learned to help you to make your reply sound convincing. You might want to use a thesaurus to help you to make your vocabulary more sophisticated. Afterwards your teacher will read out some of your replies, as well as the real one, and you will take a vote as a class as to which reply is the one from the *New Scientist*.

The question is:

> Why are dock leaves so effective at relieving stings from nettles? Are they effective on any other plant or insect stings?

The facts you need to include in your reply are:

– A nettle sting contains acid. This is what burns the skin and causes pain.

– Dock leaves contain an alkali. This neutralises the acid.

– The stings of bees and ants also contain acid so can be helped by using something containing an alkali.

– Soap and bicarbonate of soda also contain alkalis.

– Wasp stings contain alkali so you need something acidic to neutralise them, for example, vinegar.

Teachers' note: the real reply is on page 240.

Who Let the Dogs Out? & Cameras Show Who Let the Dogs Out

For this activity you will need to have read 'Who Let the Dogs Out?' and 'Cameras Show Who Let the Dogs Out'.

Before Reading

Where does the news come from?

■ In a small group brainstorm some possible answers to the question 'How does something become 'news'?'

■ Share your ideas as a class.

──────── After Reading ────────

Venn Diagram

- ■ Draw a Venn diagram, like the one below, and make a note of any similarities and differences you notice between 'Who Let the Dogs Out?' and 'Cameras Show Who Let the Dogs Out'.

- ■ With a partner, discuss what could explain the similarities between the two stories.

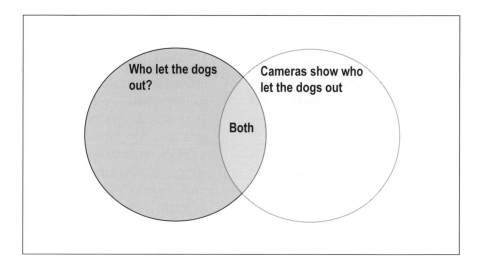

Where Does the News Come From?

- ■ As a class, read through the different sources of news on page 70.

- ■ Discuss which was the most likely source for the two stories about Red the Lurcher.

How Did this Story Become News?

The most likely source for the stories was probably a press release from Battersea Dogs and Cats Home.

- ■ Work in a group of four. Read the cards on page 70.

- ■ Take a role each and spend one minute preparing an answer to the question on your card.

- ■ In role, take it in turns to give your answer to your group.

Where does the news come from? Sources

News agencies

There are several big news agencies. They have journalists reporting to them from all over the world and these stories are put onto a computer system that other journalists can use to find the facts for a story.

Other journalists

Journalists search the web, read newspapers and magazines and watch and listen to the news. They sometimes pick up stories that have been reported elsewhere and use them in their own newspaper or news programme.

Press and publicity

Organisations such as charities, schools or government departments, and individuals such as celebrities and MPs, all want publicity. One way for them to do this is to get a story into the news. They send out what are called 'press releases' to news journalists. These are usually one page long and give information about a story the organisation or person hopes will become a news story. Journalists also get contacted by members of the public who might have had something happen to them, or hope that an event or group they are involved with might get reported in the news.

Contacts

Journalists' contacts are very precious to them – these are the people they know who can give them information on a story. A music journalist, for example, might have contacts in record companies, whereas a political journalist might know MPs or people who work for them. These insiders can give a journalist a story before anyone else knows about it, and journalists love to be first with a story.

How did this story become news? Role cards

Newspaper editor
Why did you decide to use the story?

News journalist
What did you change about the basic story to make it yours?

Press and publicity person from Battersea Dogs and Cats Home
Why did you want this story in the news?

Newspaper reader
Why did you decide to read the story?

Comparing the Stories

On the website http://answers.yahoo.com someone asked, 'What makes a good newspaper article?' A journalist's answer is reprinted on page 72.

- ■ Read the journalist's tips.

- ■ Using these tips, pull out each key point from the journalist's explanations, for example 'Hook the reader.'

- ■ As a class, agree five or six features that you think are the most important. These are now your criteria for judging the articles.

- ■ In your pair, draw a chart like the one below with the criteria you have agreed listed down the left-hand side and a column for each story. In your pair discuss how successfully each story meets the criteria. Give each story a score out of five for each criterion, with five being the best score. When you have finished, add up the scores for the two stories. Compare your grid with that of another group and compare the scores you have given.

	Who Let the Dogs Out?		Cameras Show Who Let the Dogs Out	
Criteria	Score	Why	Score	Why
Avoid clichés	1	Both stories have the same headline, which shows it is a cliché.	2	At least this headline has a slight twist on the cliché by mentioning the cameras.

———————— Your Own Writing ————————

A Comparison

- ■ You could use your grid to help you to write a comparison of the two stories. Write a paragraph about each feature and explain which story was more successful and why. You could use the phrases below to help you if you wish.

A good news story should … because… What makes story X particularly … is that …

News story X… is more… than news story Y, so…

The … of news story X is … whereas the … of news story Y is… I think Y works better because…

I like the fact that news story X … because … On the other hand, news story Y is … and I think…because…

It's important for a news story to … so that… and the worst/best news story for this is … because…

Compared with Y, news story X is less … because …

What makes a good newspaper article?

- The lead [opening paragraph] is the most important thing. If you don't hook your reader quickly, he's not going to keep reading. Short and punchy works best.

- Keep your paragraphs short – two sentences on average. That creates smaller blocks on the page, which is more appealing to the eye.

- Shorter articles tend to get read more, but sometimes it's necessary to go long, like on an enterprise or investigative story.

- Feature stories can be longer and can have longer leads. Photos help engage the reader.

- Keep in mind that some people don't read much of the article, so you want to have enough information in your first several paragraphs to satisfy them.

- If you need to, you can break up a long story with subheads. That helps a reader jump around, skip parts and digest a story.

- As the writer, you're basically the traffic cop telling the reader when to slow down and when to speed up. Excessive commas will get in the way. Semi-colons should be used rarely and exclamation marks should almost never be used.

- Don't underestimate your reader's intelligence, but don't overestimate their vocabulary. Don't try to impress them with big words that only you know the meaning of.

- Tricks like alliteration can move a reader along at a faster pace.

- Try to write like you talk but a little less informally.

- A good news story should read like poetry. It has a rhythm. Avoid overuse of conjunctions, stringing too many thoughts together, repetition of words.

- Be concise, what we call 'writing it tight'. If a word can be left out, leave it out.

- Avoid clichés.

- There are many types of writing within newspaper writing, and they're all fairly different from the many types of non-newspaper writing.

- Remember these basics: be accurate, be thorough and be done.

A Writer's View

Originality

David Almond is the author of well-known children's books such as Skellig, Heaven Eyes and The Fire-Eaters.

The word itself – ORIGINALITY – is intimidating, of course. It can hinder us before we even start. Just as abstractions like CREATIVITY and IMAGINATION can. When I was a kid, dreaming of being a writer, I used to look at my friends: 'He looks creative. She looks imaginative. But me?' And how would I write anything 'original' when already so much had been written, when I was an ordinary kid in an ordinary place. I guess I suffered, perhaps like most of us do, from the notion that creativity etc is reserved for strange exotic types, that to be truly imaginative is to be somehow superhuman. All nonsense, of course. We are wired to be creative, to tell stories. Ideas can flow spontaneously from all of us. And originality is nothing more than telling a story (which will inevitably be like some other stories) in your own way.

Writing is a discipline, but it is also a form of play, and it can be close to magic. Pick up a stone. Look at it. Feel its weight in your hand. Now tell yourself that this stone was last held by a boy called Tony Muldoon. He joyfully flung the stone aside as he ran past this place. Look at the stone. Relax, and allow the image of Tony to form in your mind. Can you see him running? What does he yell as he runs? Can you see him throw the stone? What's he running from and to? What's he wearing? What has made him so joyful? What did he dream of last night? What is his home like? Name his mother and father. The weird thing is, you know the answers. Tony comes to life in your mind. His story can grow and develop. It is a mixture of daring yourself to do it, and allowing yourself to do it. And it is strangely easy, and the more you do this kind of thing, the easier it gets. How can you do this? Because you are human, a creative being.

The beginning of writing – the empty blank page – can be very scary. The end result of writing – neat lines of black words on clean white pages – can be even more so. It all looks so neat, so accomplished, so perfect. I used to think that the writer's mind must look like this. How could I ever achieve such apparent perfection? An illusion, of course. Neat printed pages are the product of editors, typesetters, designers, printers

The creative process that leads to it is a messy, playful, sweaty, imperfect journey. Don't be intimidated. Get some marks on the page, even if they make no sense at all. All would-be writers should look at writers' notebooks and manuscripts. My own notebooks are a mess of scribble and scrawl and doodle. I spend much of my time scribbling (and enjoying scribbling) rubbish. I look through what I've scribbled and find phrases, images, notions that I like and that seem to have some strength. I lift them from the rubbish and begin to form them into sentences, paragraphs, stories. I used to try to plan and plot my stories from the start, but I can't do that. The stories grow, like living things.

Often I go into schools and ask, 'Who here writes good stories?' A couple of timid hands might be raised. Then I ask, 'Who writes awful stories?' And often there's an immediate forest of hands. It's too easy to say, 'I don't write well.' We have to train ourselves to be brave enough to say that some of our writing is really good, to find the good bits and to throw out or change the bad.

All writers are different, of course. There is no single secret or technique. But to find your own approach, it's important to experiment and play. I keep going back to the notion of play. Yes, writing can be difficult, deep etc etc but it's also a playful occupation. Play in notebooks, on scraps of paper, on envelopes. Your mind has an endless store of images, tales, memories, dreams, speculations. Relax and allow your imagination to work. Yes, have a plan/framework, but don't plan your story to death. Allow yourself to be surprised and to make discoveries as you scribble and write. Allow your story and its characters to have their own life. Don't give up after a few sentences. Write longer than you think you can. Keep going and you'll begin to be absorbed by your tale. Be brave. Enjoy yourself.

David Almond (2006)

Bits of an Autobiography I May Not Write

Two weeks of thinking, and still no idea for my next book. I'd tried everything. Meditation. Self-hypnosis. Vacuuming my scalp to stimulate my brain.

Then a letter arrived from a kid in Western Australia. 'Your books are pretty good,' she wrote, 'except for the total lack of motorbikes.'

I fell to my knees, partly in gratitude and partly because the vacuum cleaner was still on my head. At last, a story idea. A kid travelling across the Great Sandy Desert on a motorbike. Not bad.

I'd just finished chapter one when the next letter came.

'Reasonably OK books,' wrote a kid in Adelaide, 'but why so few exotic fish?'

Good point. I rewrote chapter one. It ended up longer, mostly because the bike couldn't travel so fast with the aquarium on the back.

'Your stories would be more interesting,' said a letter from Bristol, 'if they included more elderly people.'

I had to agree. I rewrote chapter one and it certainly was more interesting. Particularly when one of the kid's grandparents, parched from running to keep up with the bike, drank the aquarium and swallowed a coral trout.

It looked like she was a goner until the letter from Philadelphia arrived. 'More sports,' it said. Which is how, in the next draft, the kid came to have a table-tennis bat handy to whack Gran on the back.

'Shouldn't you be thinking up your own ideas, Dad?' asked the kids.

'Why?' I replied.

'Oh, no reason,' they shrugged, handing me six letters.

'Water-skiing,' said one. 'Clydesdale horses,' said another. 'Self-reticulating irrigation systems,' said the other four.

This morning when the postman came I hid under my desk. He found me. I was sobbing.

'Must be tough, being a writer,' he said, bending down and handing me a bundle of letters. 'I wouldn't know where to get the ideas from.'

Morris Gleitzman: Kids Night In (ed Warchild, 2003)

Writers' Tips

Several well-known children's writers give their top tips for a story writing website.

Malorie Blackman

Read! Read lots and lots of different kinds of books, picture books, graphic novels, novels, poems, newspapers, magazines. Read even the books you suspect you might not be too keen on. They're the ones which may surprise you the most. I was never keen on Westerns but then I read *Lonesome Dove* by Larry McMurtry – and it was fantastic. Once you've got an idea, think about all the ways you can make it better, more exciting, more gripping, more emotional, more real.

Tim Bowler

Just start! Sit down and get going. Lots of people put off starting until they've got the plot all worked out. I don't think that's necessary. I find the best ideas come to me while I'm actually writing. By all means chew over the story first in your head and maybe do some rough planning, but as soon as you've got some idea of what you want to say, get writing.

Anne Fine

Alan Ahlberg's joke is that the first thing to do is 'get your bum on a seat', and I'd certainly agree with that. But there is no one 'right way' to write a book. (Art is a product, not process.) So if you're a get-stuck-straight-into-it-and-fly writer, do just that. And if you're a planner and brooder, then plan and brood.

Oisin McGann

Know your ending. Make sure you're clear on where you're going before you start. You'll need a clear idea of what you want to write, of course. Make notes, plan out a basic plot, maybe even make a timeline so that you know what order things are going to happen in. I find I have to make plenty of notes, and let things find their place in the story. I give it time to stew, and when it's ready to be told, I get impatient to write it.

Make sure you have long periods of peace and quiet in which to write, so you can relax into it, and try and gradually lengthen the amount of time you can spend writing as you get into it. But the most important thing is to know your ending; it gives you something to aim at.

Bali Rai

Plan everything, even if you discard your plan halfway through. And try to think about what you are trying to say with your story. Where does it go? What do the characters think/feel? Research the areas that you aren't familiar with BEFORE you start writing. Take the time to plot your story/character development/timelines.

Narinder Dhami

Don't be in too much of a hurry to start writing. Think of an idea first to get you started. Ideas can be triggered off by anything – maybe you've seen an article in the newspaper about a family who've won the Lottery. Maybe something has happened to you personally, which you want to turn into a story. Whatever your idea, think about it for a few days before you start to write.

Catherine MacPhail

Brain storm. Jot things down, words ideas, settings, characters. Give a character a problem. I did this with *Wheels*. What was the worst problem I could give a boy ? Put him in a wheelchair. That started me thinking about how he got there. An accident? And how would he feel about that? Angry, bitter, resentful. So a character was growing in my head. And who caused the accident? Another question that needed answered, and what if I made that the mystery he has to solve to help him come to terms with what has happened to him. Sometimes, it is just a 'what if ?' that starts me off. Two boys playing on the icy loch across the street from me on a dark afternoon. What if the ice broke? What if they were on an isolated loch with no one watching? What if there was only one boy and not two? And *Dark Waters* started to form in my mind. Grab hold of an idea, jot it down and it is trapped on the paper, then you can work on it.

Celia Rees

Collect ideas. Keep a notebook and jot down anything that catches your interest, or might make a good story. Collect photos, postcards, newspaper cuttings, too – stick them in your book as reminders and stimuli. After a while, you'll find that your notebook contains lots of starting points for your own, original stories.

From www.storiesontheweb.org
A Reader Development Project,
Birmingham Libraries

How the Water Feels to the Fishes

Like the fur of a chinchilla. Like the cleanest tooth. Yes, the fishes say, this is what it feels like. People always ask the fishes, 'What does the water feel like to you?' and the fishes are always happy to oblige. Like feathers are to other feathers, they say. Like powder touching ash. When the fishes tell us these things, we begin to understand. We begin to think we know what the water feels like to the fishes. But it's not always like fur and ash and the cleanest tooth. At night, they say, the water can be different. At night, when it's very cold, it can be like the tongue of a cat. At night, when it's very very cold, the water is like cracked glass. Or honey. Or forgiveness, they say, ha ha. When the fishes answer these questions – which they are happy to do they also ask why. They are curious, fish are, and thus they ask, Why? Why do you want to know what the water feels like to the fishes? And we are never quite sure. The fishes press further. Do you breathe air? they ask. The answer, we say, is yes. Well then, they say, What does the air feel like to you? And we do not know. We think of air and we think of wind, but that's another thing. Wind is air in action, air on the move, and the fishes know this. Well then, they ask again, what does the air feel like? And we have to think about this. Air feels like air, we say, and the fishes laugh mirthlessly. Think! they say. Think, they say, now gentler. And we think and we guess that it feels like hair, thousands of hairs, swaying ever so slightly in breezes microscopic. The fishes laugh again. Do better, think harder, they say. It feels like language, we say, and they are impressed. Keep going, they say. It feels like blood, we say, and they say, No, no, that's not it. The air is like being wanted, we say, and they nod approvingly. The air is like getting older, they say, and they touch our arms gently.

Dave Eggers: How the Water Feels to the Fishes (2007)

A Writer's View
Activities

Originality

━━━━━ Before Reading ━━━━━

Creative Qualities 1

■ Think of something you are creative at, for example:

- cooking
- football
- creating an outfit
- daydreaming
- writing stories
- dancing
- thinking of excuses for why you haven't done your homework.

■ Use the prompts below to help you to come up with the three qualities you think are the most important in being creative.

- Taking a risk
- Feeling confident
- Being talented
- Experimenting

- Not sticking to the rules
- Not caring what other people think
- Working hard
- Being daring.

———————————— **After Reading** ————————————

Creative Qualities 2

■　As a class, discuss what qualities David Almond seems to think make someone creative.

———————————— **Your Own Writing** ————————————

A big company once employed some researchers to study various people who were considered to be very creative in their jobs. They wanted to know if studying what qualities these people had would provide useful information to help other people to be creative. When the researchers had finished their study, they concluded that the only thing all the creative people had in common was the fact that they believed they were creative. Thinking they were creative seemed to be the key to being creative! This is worth bearing in mind as you do the next activity.

The Stone and Tony Muldoon

Working with a partner, you are going to use David Almond's advice to help you to get ideas for a story. Then you are going to write the opening of the story.

1. Gathering ideas

■　In your pair, decide who is A and who is B.

■　B's: you are going to try to follow David Almond's instructions on getting ideas for a story by imagining what happens to a stone. Your partner is going to read the instructions to you twice. As they do so, close your eyes, listen, and try to do as Almond suggests.

■　A's: read the extract from the text (on page 83) to your partner slowly, twice.

■　B's: when your partner has finished reading, open your eyes but do not say anything to your partner. You have one minute to write some notes to help you to remember the ideas you had while your partner was reading. You could just write key words, or you could write whole phrases, it is up to you.

■　Swap roles so that the B's now take the role of readers.

Extract

Writing is a discipline, but it is also a form of play, and it can be close to magic. Pick up a stone. Look at it. Feel its weight in your hand. Now tell yourself that this stone was last held by a boy called Tony Muldoon. He joyfully flung the stone aside as he ran past this place. Look at the stone. Relax, and allow the image of Tony to form in your mind. Can you see him running? What does he yell as he runs? Can you see him throw the stone? What's he running from and to? What's he wearing? What has made him so joyful? What did he dream of last night? What is his home like? Name his mother and father. The weird thing is, you know the answers. Tony comes to life in your mind. His story can grow and develop. It is a mixture of daring yourself to do it, and allowing yourself to do it. And it is strangely easy, and the more you do this kind of thing, the easier it gets. How can you do this? Because you are human, a creative being.

2. Writing your opening

■ Use your notes to help you to write three different possible openings to a story called 'The Stone and Tony Muldoon'. You should write between one and four paragraphs. Use David Almond's advice:

I look through what I've scribbled and find phrases, images, notions that I like and that seem to have some strength. I lift them from the rubbish and begin to form them into sentences, paragraphs, stories.

■ Share your openings with your partner and get their advice about what they like best in each opening.

■ Write a final draft opening, making use of your best ideas and the advice from your partner.

———— Extension Work ————

The Whole Story

■ Continue on from your opening to write the story of 'The Stone and Tony Muldoon', trying to keep all of your writing up to the quality of the opening.

■ Or, use your partner's opening and continue it to write the rest of the story, again trying to keep all of your writing up to the quality of the opening.

Bits of an Autobiography I May Not Write

——— Before Reading ———

The Ideas Shop

■ Writers are always being asked, 'Where do you get your ideas from?' The poet Brian Pattern answered '…there is a little shop down a back alley in Liverpool; it is a tiny place full of wonderful ideas; they have gigantic jars full of them, some are blue, others are golden, some glitter, some simply shimmer and others are very quiet and some are even a bit dull. Anyway, I get my ideas from this shop…'

■ Work in pairs and take it in turns to play the parts of a writer being interviewed and the interviewer. The interviewer should ask the writer 'Where do you get your ideas from?' The writer should answer in role, but can choose to take the question seriously, or give a fanciful answer, like Brian Patten.

■ As a class, share some of the more interesting answers.

——— After Reading ———

How is this Text Like a Joke?

The joke on page 85 is what is called a shaggy dog story, a kind of long-winded joke with lots of detail building to a punch-line. The punch-line is usually the kind which makes the listener groan, rather than laugh. The pleasure for the joke teller is to keep people listening for as long as possible, because they are expecting a laugh at the end.

■ Read the shaggy dog story on page 85, or share shaggy dog stories you know in your class, then answer the questions that follow.

■ With a partner, discuss in what ways 'Bits of an Autobiography I May Not Write' is similar to a shaggy dog story, and in what ways it is different.

■ Feed back your ideas to the class.

A Shaggy Dog Story

Four brothers left home for university, one after the other. Each one was successful and made lots of money. Meeting up just before the 70th birthday of their mother, who lived in a far away city, they discussed the gifts that they were planning to send her.

The first said, 'I've had a twenty room mansion built for her, she will move in on the day of her birthday.' The second said, 'I'm paying for a fifty seat cinema to be built in the basement of the mansion.' The third said, 'I'm having my Mercedes dealer deliver her an SL600 on the morning of her birthday.' The fourth said, 'Listen to this. You know how mum loved reading the Bible but she can't read it anymore because she can't see very well? I met a priest who told me about a parrot that can recite the entire Bible. It took twenty priests 12 years to teach him. I had to pledge to contribute £100,000 a year for twenty years to the church, but it was worth it. She just has to name the chapter and verse and the parrot will recite it.' The other brothers were impressed.

After her birthday, mum sent out her 'Thank You' notes.

She wrote:
'Richard, the house you built is so huge. I live in only one room, but I have to clean the whole house. Thanks anyway.'

'Peter, I am too old to travel. I stay at home and have my shopping delivered, so I never use the Mercedes. The thought was good, though. Thanks.'

'Michael, you gave me an expensive cinema with Dolby sound. It can hold 50 people. But all my friends are dead, I've lost my hearing and I'm nearly blind. I'll never use it. Thank you for the gesture just the same.'

'Dearest Christopher, you were the only son to have the good sense to give a little thought to your gift. The chicken was delicious. Thank you.'

Writers' Tips

After Reading

Writing to Advise

■ You are going to work with a partner to turn the tips given by these writers into a leaflet to help other students your age to improve their story writing.

1. Structuring your leaflet

Below you will find 15 possible headings to use in your leaflet.

■ With a partner, decide which headings would be the most useful. You should narrow the list down to between four and eight headings. Use the prompts that follow to help you to make your decision.

- Which headings would students find most useful?

- Have you chosen a spread of headings to cover different stages or aspects of the writing process?

- Check back in the text – is there useful information from at least one writer for each of the headings you have chosen?

Getting ideas	Beginnings	Endings	Planning	Setting
Getting started	Character	Plot	Your noteboook	Your own reading
Openings	Middles	Before you start	Reflection time	Research

2. Deciding what to include

■ With your partner, use the headings you have chosen to make notes about the advice each writer gives for this section of your leaflet. You can change your headings if necessary as you work.

■ Look over your notes and discuss which tips students would find most interesting and useful. Cross out anything you are definitely not going to use.

Some of the writers say things that contradict each other, for example, Bali Rai says always plan, whereas Tim Bowler says just get started.

■ Look at the following ways to deal with this problem and discuss the pros and cons of each suggestion before deciding on the approach, or combination of approaches you will take. You could:

– keep the advice simple by choosing only one point of view for each heading

– use only the advice from writers whose books you like

– list several different ways of doing things under each heading

– use quotes from the writers to show that the advice comes from different people with different ways of working

– explain what the different suggestions are and then advise which way you think is best.

3. Setting out your leaflet

■ Think about how to set out your leaflet to make it eye catching and appealing to students and draw a rough version to plan how to present your information. You could include:

– headings and sub-headings

– bullet points, boxes and/or bold text for key points

– larger fonts/size of writing for headings

– pictures, photographs, cartoons or diagrams

– columns

– a logo and/or slogan.

4. Writing your leaflet

■ Write your leaflet, keeping in mind your target audience. As you write you will need to consider:

– how to keep your readers interested

– how to persuade them to use your advice

– how to make your key points clear and memorable

– how to give clear advice without being bossy.

How the Water Feels to the Fishes

———————— Before Reading ————————

A Writer's Problem

Dave Eggers thought it would be interesting to write about what the water feels like to the fishes.

■ With a partner, discuss what problems this might give you, as writers.

■ Now discuss what solutions you might be able to come up with to solve the problems.

■ Share your possible problems and solutions as a class.

■ Now read the first two sentences of the text, below. With a partner discuss the questions that follow.

– What kind of text do you think this is going to be? What makes you think this?

– Do you get any hint as to how Dave Eggers has solved the problem of how to describe what the water feels like to the fishes? Is it a solution that you and your partner had thought of?

> L ike the fur of a chinchilla. Like the cleanest tooth.

■ Now read these similes from the same text. What do you think is being described (it is *not* what the water feels like to the fishes)?

> …it feels like hair, thousands of hairs, swaying ever so slightly in breezes microscopic.

> It feels like language.

> It feels like blood.

After Reading

Your Response

■ Think to yourself for a moment about your response to the text. What did it make you think or feel? Share your thoughts with the person sitting next to you.

Solutions to the Writer's Problem

■ With a partner, discuss how Dave Eggers solved some or all of the problems you came up with. Are there any you don't think he solved successfully?

Your Own Writing

Unusual Descriptions

You are going to do a short piece of writing describing something unusual.

■ Choose from one of the ideas below. Before you start writing, brainstorm possible writing problems and possible solutions, remembering what you have learned from the way Dave Eggers described how the water feels to the fishes.

  – How the air feels to the birds.

  – How the earth feels to the worms.

  – How hair feels to the headlice.

  – How the cold feels to the penguins.

You might like to write your final piece of writing as a short story (like Dave Eggers). Or you may prefer to present it as a poem. It's up to you.

Working with More than One Text

For this activity you will need to have read 'Writers' Tips' and either 'Originality' or 'Bits of an Autobiography I May Not Write', or both.

──────── Your Own Writing ────────

■ Write a short piece describing what usually happens when you write a story. Think about the prompts below before you start writing.

– You could write this as a humorous, autobiographical piece, like Morris Gleitzman, or as a serious piece.

– Include things like how (or whether) you plan, where you get your ideas from, and so on.

– Whichever style you choose, show or explain which bits of your writing process are successful, and which bits you struggle with.

Ties That Bind

The Birthday Cake

Just Like Your Father

Begi-Begi and Jill-Jilli

Treasure's Pocket Money

Treasure's Pocket Money

Gina Davidson's articles about her teenage daughter first appeared as a column in the Guardian.

Treasure was born to spend. She therefore needs huge amounts of pocket money. It is her life blood, she can scarcely move without it. She spends it, lends it, donates it, loses it. She buys snacks, tickets, make-up, bargain offers and presents. She is a fountain of pocket money and I am the source of her wealth – the magic porridge pot. Treasure says the correct words and up comes more pocket money. Because without it she is a prisoner in the house, an unpleasant option for both of us.

'I must have some,' she begs. 'I need it. I had to pay all the taxi fare because no one else had any money. They're all going to pay me back.'

'Good. Then you'll have some money.'

'But I haven't got enough money to *get* to them.' Treasure is at her wits' end. 'You don't understand how much I spend on fares.' She is addressing an ignoramus. 'Fares are very expensive.' Her needs are always pressing. This month has been particularly pressing because it was Peter's birthday and Chloe's birthday *and* she had to buy Easter eggs.

I am keen to know how much pocket money her friends get. Treasure doesn't know. Her friends don't know either. They become confused when asked. They don't even remember whether they have to earn it by doing the odd household task. This is a mysterious grey area.

Treasure is meant to do certain chores to earn her money. She doesn't refuse. She will do them, she promises, but she has other more urgent duties – dancing in her room, hugging the dog, phoning Rosie, going to sleep. In my weak way I have not always enforced these rules. Naturally people have criticised. 'You're making a rod for your own back,' bellows Grandma. She compares her indolent grandchild to the girls who used to live next door. They were paragons in Grandma's eyes. They peeled potatoes, made beds, washed up, never answered back. Having given up on me, Grandma tries Treasure.

'There's only one thing I want you to do,' she begs Treasure in a tragic way. 'Just help your mother. That's all I want you to do.'

This request always throws Treasure into a sullen fury. Grandma's wishes have never been realised. I continue to dole out pocket money regardless. But at least Treasure is a generous child. She spends the bulk of it on presents. I do rather well out of her pocket money. I even have a Teasmade. I have chocs, flowers, tapes and my birthdays are sumptuous affairs. Nevertheless I have cut the pocket money now and then when Treasure's behaviour has gone beyond the pale. But that ploy no longer works. Treasure has a new ally. The bank.

The wicked bank tempted Treasure with a cash card and tons of free gifts. It advertised on TV. All her saved up birthday and Christmas present money can now be frittered with ease. The bank is eager for Treasure to join our nation of debtors and be one of them. It does not wish to encourage thrift. I am no match for such an opponent. I dream that one day, when all Treasure's savings are gone and I am bankrupt, necessity will force me to be strict about pocket money.

Treasure must have read my mind. 'I don't want you to give me all my pocket money,' says she out of the blue. 'I want to save it. I want you to put it in this piggy bank in your room so I can't get it.' She stuffs a fiver into the pig. 'Can I have some advance pocket money? I need three pounds. I must have it.'

'But you've got that five.'

'I can't spend that,' says Treasure. 'I'm saving it.'

Gina Davidson: Treasure – the Trials of a Teenage Terror (1999)

The Birthday Cake

The air was cold and the daylight was draining from the sky. The street smelled of rotten fruit left in the carts and although this was a sour smell it was not altogether unpleasant. Lucia was accustomed to this odor, and because it reminded her of the feast days when she was a girl she enjoyed it, the way she imagined people on farms enjoyed the smell of manure.

It was past six and the shops on Newbury Street were closed, but she knew that Lorenzo would stay open for her. She did not hurry: she was an old woman, and age had spoiled her legs. They were thick now, and water heavy, and when she walked her hips grew sore from the effort of moving them.

She stopped by a bench, wanting to sit but knowing that to stoop and then to rise would be more difficult than simply to lean against the backrest. She waited for her breathing to slow, then walked the last block to the bakery. Lorenzo would be there. He would wait. Hadn't she come to the bakery every Saturday since the war? And hadn't she bought the same white cake with chocolate frosting, Nico's favorite?

'Buona sera[1]. Signora Ronsavelli,' he said as the chime clanged and the heavy glass door closed behind her. 'You had me concerned.'

Lorenzo Napoli was too young to be so worried all the time. She wondered about him. She did not trust him the way she had trusted his father.

Standing before the pastry case was Maria Mendez, the little Puerto Rican girl who worked at the laundry. 'Este es la señora[2],' Lorenzo said to her. They were everywhere now, these Puerto Ricans, all over the neighborhood with their loud cars and shouting children and men drinking beer on the sidewalk. Now the rents were increasing and the real estate people wanted the Italians to move to nursing homes. Even Father D'Agostino was helping them. 'Lucia,' the priest had told her, 'you'd have company there.'

This Maria from the laundry had a child but no husband. She smiled at Lucia, then peered down into the glass case.

'Miss Mendez needs to ask you a favor,' the baker said.

[1] *Buona sera = Good evening.*
[2] *Este es la señora = This is the lady.*

94

Lucia removed her leather gloves and put them into her purse. 'A favor?'

'My little girl,' Maria said. 'Today is her birthday. She's seven years old today.'

'You must know little Teresa,' Lorenzo said.

'Yes,' Lucia said. She had indeed seen the child, out with her friends tearing up the vegetable gardens in the backyards.

'And I was so busy today at the laundry, so busy, all day long there was a line, and I couldn't get out to buy her a birthday cake.'

'Yes.' Lucia remembered that it had taken her two days to fix the stakes for her tomato plants.

'Let me explain,' Lorenzo said. 'Miss Mendez needs a cake and I have none left, except yours. I told her that you were my best customer, and of course we'd have to wait and ask you.'

'All the other bakeries are closed,' Maria said. 'It's my little girl's birthday.'

Lucia's hands began to shake. She remembered what the doctor had said about getting angry; but this was too much. 'Every week I buy my cake. For how many years? And now this *muli* comes in and you just give it away?'

'Lucy.' Lorenzo held out his hands like a little boy.

'Don't get angry. Please, Lucy.'

'No. Not Lucy.' She tapped her chest with her finger. 'Lucia.'

'Lucy, please,' he said.

'No 'Please, Lucy.' Non parlare Inglese[1]. Italiano.'

'I could give you some sugar cookies,' he said. 'Or some cannolis[2]. I just made them. They're beautiful.'

'Once a week I come here and I buy Nico's cake.'

Lorenzo tipped his head to the side. He seemed to be about to say something, but then he stopped. He waited another moment.

'Lucia, think of the poor little girl,' he said. 'It's her birthday.'

'Then bake her a cake. You do the favor, if you like her so much.'

'Lucia, there's no time.' The party was going to begin in a few minutes, he said. Besides, he had already cleaned his equipment and put away his flour and eggs and sugar.

---

[1] *Non palare Inglese. Italiano. = Don't speak English. Italian.'*
[2] *A traditional Italian pastry: a crisp pastry tube with a creamy filling*

'Lucia,' he said, 'it's the right thing. Ask yourself, what would Nico do? Or my father?'

'I know what they wouldn't do. They wouldn't forget who their people were. They wouldn't start speaking Spanish for the *mulis*.'

She stared at him until he looked away. Outside, the wind had lifted a newspaper from the sidewalk and was pressing the leaves against the front window of the bakery. From somewhere on Common Street came the sound of a car's engine racing. She thought of Nico, how when he lay sick in bed during his last days she had gone outside and asked the children not to make noise and they'd laughed and told her to go on back inside, crazy old lady.

Without looking up, he spoke in a voice that was almost a whisper. 'Lucia,' he said, 'it's just this once.'

'No,' she said. 'No. I want my cake.'

Maria began to cry. 'Dios mio,' she said. 'My little girl.'

Lorenzo leaned on his hands. 'I'm sorry, Miss Mendez.'

Maria turned to her. She was sobbing. 'It's my daughter's birthday,' she said. 'How will she forgive me? Don't you have children?'

'I have three children,' Lucia said. 'And I never forgot their birthdays. I never had to rush out at the last minute.'

'I was working,' Maria said. 'I'm all by myself with Teresa. I have to raise her alone.'

'And whose fault is that?' Lucia waved at Lorenzo. 'Pronto[1],' she said. 'Box up my cake.'

Lorenzo eased the cake out of the display case and placed it into a white cardboard pastry box. His hands were soft and white. He drew a length of twine from the dispenser, tied off the box, then snapped his wrists and broke the string from the leader.

Lucia put on her gloves. As she turned for the door Maria took her arm. 'I'll beg you,' she said. 'Please, I'll buy the cake from you. I'll pay you ten dollars.'

Lucia pulled her arm free. 'I don't want your money.'

'Twenty dollars, then.' She pulled a folded bill from the pocket of her dress and placed it in Lucia's hand. 'Please, Mrs. Ronsavelli, take it.'

Lucia tried to push the bill back into her hands, but Maria curled her fingers into fists and began to cry. 'You can't do this,' she said.

Lucia threw the crumpled bill to the floor and opened the door. Maria fell to her

[1] *Pronto = quickly*

knees and picked up the bill. 'You witch!' she screamed. 'Puta! Whore!'

Lucia did not look back. She moved slowly down Newbury Street, being careful to avoid the spots of ice. What did that laundry girl, or even Lorenzo, understand about her? What did they know about devotion?

From the alley behind her building she heard the screaming, a terrible choked wail that rang from the street and into the alley and echoed off the walls and trash cans. She imagined Maria the laundress stumbling home to her daughter, and she imagined the red, contorted face of the little girl when her friends arrived and there was no cake.

Still, what would they know about suffering, even then? They would know nothing. The light was poor in the staircase, and she held the railing with her free hand. After each step she paused; she let the flicker of pain ease from her hips, then lifted again.

Inside the kitchen she raised the glass cover and took out last week's cake. The air that had been under the glass smelled sweet and ripe. The cake had not been touched; it might have been a clay model of the new one. As she carried it to the trash, tips of chocolate frosting broke off and scattered on the floor like shards of pottery.

She swept up the pieces, washed the smudges of frosting from the cake stand with a sponge, then opened the bakery box, removed the new cake and put it under the glass cover. It was dark outside, and in the hills around the city the lights in the windows of hundreds of houses glowed like the tiny white bulbs in the branches of a Christmas tree. She thought of her children; they were up in those hills, eating dinner with their own children – those little light-skinned boys and girls who shrank from their nana's hugs, kept their jackets on, and whispered to each other until it was time to leave. It was cold near the window; she shivered and stepped away.

She sat at the kitchen table, beneath the photos of Nico and the children. She looked at the door, wishing, as she did each time, that there might be a knock, or that it might just swing open, and one of them, just one of them, might be there.

Daniel Lyons: Birthday Stories (ed Haruki Murakami, 2006)

Just Like Your Father

'**Y**ou're just like your father!'

I stared at Mum.

She stared at me. She looked taken aback, as if someone else had taken control of her mouth.

'That's a stupid thing to say.'

'I know,' said Mum. 'I didn't mean it. It's just... I don't know who you are any more sometimes, Josh.'

'I don't know either,' I said miserably. I plucked at the sleeves of my sweatshirt. They no longer covered my long bony wrists. 'I need a new one, Mum.'

'But I only got you that one at Christmas. And it wasn't half a price, too.'

Mum gently prodded the designer lettering. I didn't have the heart to tell her it wasn't cool any more, that these very initials spelt nerd and naff this month. I concentrated on unarguable fact.

'It's too small.'

Mum tried pulling it down, like I was a toddler who hadn't quite got the knack of dressing himself.

'Leave it out, Mum!' I said, wriggling free.

'It *is* too small,' she said, sighing, folding her arms as she looked at me. Looked *up* at me.

For the past year I'd been able to see the top of her head. It was weird noticing the little pink patch where her hair parted too determinedly, and the dark mouse of her roots. She tried so hard to keep herself looking good. When she went off with her women friends on Friday nights, all dolled up in too-tight clothes, I got a lump in my throat.

It was worse when she came back at eleven, talking brightly, telling me she'd had a really great night out when she looked so tired and her plum lipstick was smudged.

98

Not with kissing. Mum never seemed to meet up with any men. She said she didn't want to, didn't need a man in her life. She used to say, 'You're the only man for me, Josh.' But that was when I was a little kid.

'You're too big,' she said.

'What?'

'It's you, not the sweatshirt,' Mum said, smiling to show it was a joke. 'When are you going to stop growing?'

'*I* don't know,' I said. 'I wish you wouldn't keep going on about it.'

I was getting a complex. I'd always been a bit on the small side. Mum often called me Little Titch. We were both sure I took after her. I had her dark-mouse hair and her brown eyes and her neat wiry body. She could still run like the wind for a bus even in her high heels, or vacuum the house from top to bottom, dancing along to her daft old eighties albums, not even out of breath. I'd never been much of a dancer (I was strictly a guy who leant against the wall at the school disco) but I could run fast enough to make the first three on sports day and I was in Mr Townsend's first team for football, which came in useful to establish my Lad credibility.

I had to work hard to avoid any Mummy's Boy taunts. When I was young and stupid I'd burble on about Mum and me going swimming on Saturdays, or Mum and me going up to the Trocadero for a treat, or Mum and me sharing a pizza with six extra toppings for our Sunday lunch. The other kids would roll their eyes and go 'Mum-and-me' in silly prissy voices.

I'd learnt to shut up about Mum and me. Not that we did that much together nowadays. Not that I did anything much with anyone. I moseyed around by myself or lay on my bed for hours, staring, wondering if one day I was going to graze the ceiling when I stood up. **‖**

I'd grown six inches in the last six months and I didn't show any sign of stopping. I wondered if my body would ever cotton on that it had grown enough. Maybe my arms would carry on until I could reach all the way up the road and round the corner and my legs would stretch until I could see clear over every tower block and have to bat the birds out of my way.

My head and torso couldn't quite catch up and my shoulders were hunched anyway because I'd started to feel permanently defensive. Mr Townsend wanted me to go along to this gym to work out.

'It's time you developed that growing body, lad. You want to look like a gorilla, not a giraffe.'

I wasn't inspired by either animal, and I was wary of Mr Townsend. He'd never done anything dodgy but I knew he wasn't the sort of guy who liked girls. I didn't act like I was either. I blushed like a beetroot and ran backwards whenever any of the girls at school so much as spoke to me, and I never joined in all the jolly tits-and-bums talk with the other boys in my class – but in bed at nights I thought about girls a lot. That was another worrying area of growth.

There was so much physical activity going on in my body I felt that any minute now I'd go 'twang' like elastic. It didn't help that Mum kept hassling me. Like, 'Do you have to lounge there like a great lump? Couldn't you even put the potatoes on for us? I wouldn't *mind* if you were doing your homework or some kind of hobby. Why don't you have hobbies any more? But it really gets on my nerves when you just lie on that sofa waiting for me to come home from work to fetch and run for you.'

She rabbited on like this and I tried to stare straight past her and concentrate on the wallpaper because it seemed the more peaceful option. She got madder and madder, thumping things around in the kitchen and flexing her arms ostentatiously because she's always scared she'll get Repetitive Strain Injury with all the keyboard work at her Building Society. I made the mistake of yawning in the middle of her sentence. I wasn't being deliberately rude, I was *tired*, but I suppose it looked a little insulting. And that was when she came right out and said it.

'You're just like your father!'

The words seemed to have jammed in my brain. I didn't have a clue what my father was like – apart from the fact that he was an all-time Mr Bad Guy. He left when I was three, right after my mum miscarried my brother-who-never-was. I wish he'd been born. I'd give anything to have a brother, even if we fought all the time. At least it would break up this Mum-and-me thing a bit. But we *were* just Mum-and-me, and Dad had done a runner with some eighteen year old at his work and never bothered to get in touch. Well, once or twice at Christmas. He didn't ever remember birthdays, but there was a full Manchester United football strip when I was about eight – though it was a very little kid's size, so I couldn't wear it without looking ridiculous.

Then there was one of those huge floppy polar bears, grubby round the paws like it had been hanging about a fairground for a few months first. A great mangy toy bear for a boy going on ten. Mum hauled it off to the Oxfam shop the first day it opened after Christmas and I didn't try to stop her – but I missed that bear a lot. When Mum was out in the kitchen basting our mini turkey-for-two I lugged the bear off the floor and buried my face in its off-white nylon fur. Not to hug the *bear*. To try to sniff out some strange smell – an unfamiliar aftershave, cigarettes, booze. I had no idea what my dad smelt like. But the bear smelt synthetically of itself, no help at all.

Mum wasn't much help either. She mostly didn't mention Dad – or when I badgered her she'd speak in jerky little sentences, her face screwed up, as if the words were glass splinters on her tongue. He had curly hair. He had a funny laugh. He liked a drink. When I got older, especially after she'd had a drink or two herself, she'd tell me what he was *really* like: the good looks, the flirting, the drinking – the violence too. She never said, but I sometimes wondered if he'd had anything to do with my brother's miscarriage. I knew he'd not been a great dad with me. He hadn't been *any* kind of a dad.

He hadn't sent presents recently. Not even cards. On my last birthday I didn't even wonder whether there'd be anything from Dad. I didn't *want* anything. I'd cut him out of my life for ever.

But now he seemed to be creeping in through *me*. I'd always thought I had straight hair but when I worried that my crew cut emphasized my new pinhead I discovered my hair grew curly when it got the chance. Mum said she didn't know who I was any more – but we both knew. I was turning into a guy just like my dad and I couldn't stand it.

'I'm going out for a bit, Mum,' I said, suddenly desperate to get out of the house.

'Where? What are you on about? Your tea's nearly ready.'

'I know. I'm sorry. I just… I've got to go *out*.'

I went before she could stop me, striding off purposefully though I didn't really have a clue where I was going. I felt mean about Mum. She looked like she was crying when I slammed out of the door. Just like my father. Give me another few years and perhaps I'd be living out my night fantasies. Would I then get some girl into trouble and hit her and yell at her little kid and walk out on them for ever and break their hearts?

I felt as bad as if I'd actually done it already. I kept catching glimpses of myself in shop fronts and car windows until there seemed to be hundreds of big boy-men patrolling the pavements with me, all of them huge, all of them hateful.

I wished I could stop growing. I wished I could shrink back into being a really little kid. Maybe if I'd been a really cute cheeky little chap, Dad might have stayed after all. Maybe he'd have taken me to the park to feed the ducks, and kicked a football about with me, and set me on his knee at nights and told me a story – a fairy story about a beast who was tamed by a little boy so he turned into the handsome prince. ▮▮

I found I was walking right up to the park gates, as if my big feet with their ever-growing toes crammed up tight inside their trainers had a will of their own. So I gave in and walked once round the park, wishing I had some stale bread for the ducks.

There was a little gaggle of girls from my school looking around, quacking louder than the ducks, and when they spotted me they started calling out silly stuff.

'Hey, Josh!'

'Golly gosh, Josh!'

'Where you going, Josh?'

'Come and walk with us, Josh.'

'What's the weather like up there, Josh?'

'What's that on your head, Josh?'

Like a fool I felt my hair. They all shrieked.

'It's a *cloud*, Josh!'

I bared my teeth in a foolish Snoopy grin and rushed right past them, hot all over though it was a dank day and getting even chillier now it was nearly dark.

I sloped off to the kids' playground and sat on a swing, scraping the toes of my trainers backwards and forwards. The playground was empty at first, all the mums and kids gone home for tea. Then this guy came trailing along with a big baby in a buggy. At first glance you'd think he'd be more likely taking a Rottweiler for a walk. The guy was big and brawny and it was a safe bet there were tattoos somewhere under his sweatshirt. He was getting on a bit, his hair greying, his face lined. I wasn't sure if he was Dad or Grandad. He was obviously someone really special to the baby. It was grinning gummily up at him. I didn't know if it was a boy or a girl because it was all wrapped up in its jacket and little dungarees. It had a bag of bread in its damp woolly mittens and it kept on going, 'Quack quack.'

'Yes, quack quack. The ducks go quack quack,' said the man patiently, though he'd obviously said it thirty or forty times since leaving the pond.

'Quack quack,' said the baby.

'Yes, quack quack. You're the little duck. Let's take you home and feed you, little duck, it's getting dark and cold.'

'Quack quack!' said the baby, but then it caught sight of the swings and started wailing.

'No, you don't want a swing now, chum, we've got to go home,' said the man. 'Come on, quack quack.'

But the quack game was out of fashion now. The baby's wail said swing swing swing with increasing urgency.

'Okay, okay, one little swing and then we *must* go home,' said the man.

He patiently unbuckled, unstrapped and unhooked and then sat on the swing himself with the squirmy baby on his lap, gently moving to and fro, to and fro.

We were around the same height so our eyes kept meeting. The man grinned a little foolishly.

'Kids,' he said.　**❚❚**

I nodded, as if I were knowledgeable in that area. I wanted to talk some more. I wanted to get to know all about this tall tough guy. I wanted to find out if he really was the grandad. Maybe he was a second-time-around dad and putting in more time with this kid. I thought about my own missing dad.

In the end I didn't say anything. We both swung backwards and forwards and the baby squeaked with delight, waving its soggy mittens in the air. It wailed again when the man eventually bundled it back into the buggy, but then he distracted it with some more duck imitations and they quacked-quacked off together into the dark.

I sat on for a bit, thinking. If the two of them hadn't got on it wouldn't have been the baby's fault. And maybe it wouldn't have been all the guy's fault either. But they did get on. They were a great father and son. I'd had a lousy father but it didn't mean I had to be a lousy father later on.

All this thinking was doing my head in. I decided it was time to make for home too. The girls were still messing around by the duckpond.

I decided to get in before they did. I called out, 'Hey there, little munchkins,' and made them giggle some more. I still blushed, but it was so dark they couldn't see.

All the spring flowers scented the night. I bent over quickly and plucked a handful to give to Mum when I got back. I strode home in my seven league trainers, happy to have my head in the clouds.

Jacqueline Wilson: The Family Tree (ed Miriam Hodgson, 1993)

Begi-begi and Jill-jillie

Dad disappeared when I was seven. My mum said he treated us cruelly and my sister and I could see that she worked very hard, cleaning people's houses, looking after other people's children during the day and sometimes baby-sitting them into the night. The flat was always noisy with the sound of crying babies. My little sister may have forgotten our dad, but for me he was always there. I could see his hands, feel his presence. He was gone, of course. He had left us, but secretly, without ever saying it to Mum or to Sonia my sister, I felt, as if by magic, he was with us.

You see, Dad was a magician. A real one. But he was strange because he said he didn't believe in magic. Like God; who doesn't believe in God? He used to show me, when we were only five and four years old, how to do a few tricks myself. He did this trick of the 'two-headed-coin'. You hold a pound coin in your right hand and show your audience that it's heads up. Then you slap it onto your left hand and move your right hand away and it's still heads. It hasn't flipped over. My friends are still intrigued by the trick and try and grab the coin to see if it's really a coin with two heads. Of course it isn't. You have to learn the trick of letting the coin fall under its own weight and not be twisted by your turning hand.

He always said he wanted me to grow up to be a scientist so he'd show me tricks, which he could explain with science, like balancing two forks on the edge of a glass by hanging them on a fifty pence piece. It looks like magic but it isn't. And he used to tell me that all magic had its explanations. The audience mustn't be told that, and it would spoil the fun to tell me how the tricks worked, but that I was family and within the family we had to know that there was no such thing as magic.

At my seventh birthday party he did some very good tricks. We lived in a house with a garden and I invited my friends from school and Dad gave them a magic show. He was doing shows all over the country then and his assistant Clara used to sit in the box and be cut in two. She came to the party too and they weren't going to do that trick at all, but then my sister, who was five, kept shouting, 'Cut Clara up, cut Clara up,' and when I told my friends what she was saying they crowded round my dad and asked him if he could cut the lady in two. He did. Clara got changed into her costume which was kept in our magic garage and they brought the box out and turned on the music tape and everyone was amazed when she came out in one piece, dancing.

Dad did the snake trick, letting his snakes out of the jar and making them disappear when all the kids screamed and scrambled. The snakes slithered out of the jar and the kids started to run out when my dad asked them what they were frightened of and they said the snakes.

'Where? What snakes?' he said and when we looked the snakes were all in the jar again. They all thought that was so cool.

He used to say, 'Begi-begi and jill-jillie,' before making things appear or disappear. It was the spell he used.

'Why don't you say 'abracadabra', like other magicians?' I asked him.

'Because the power of 'begi-begi' is much greater than the power of 'abracadabra'. It's older and stronger and more mysterious,' he said.

So that was the spell I used at nights, kneeling by my bed and praying with all my might to the powers that made magic work, to try and get him back. Just after he went missing my mum told us that he was on tour and he would be coming back. We were used to his being away for a few days and even for a week or two when it was a long engagement at the seaside in summer. But this time he didn't come back and it became clear to me that he didn't intend to return home and to us. He must have phoned Mum or told her and I knew she missed him and wanted him back, but she didn't want to show us that she was sad.

I don't know how long it was after he left that she told us that Dad had gone back to India, that he still loved us but he wanted to be on his own to think things out. I didn't understand what she meant. What I imagined was Dad climbing a bare mountain with a bundle on his back, quite alone with no one for miles and miles around, walking and 'thinking things out'.

After he'd gone we stopped hopping from town to town and from flat to flat like we had before. I remember moving in those days, before I was seven, from London, to Swindon, to Glasgow and other places I don't remember. We moved, my mum said, because Dad had to get work in different places. My mum moved my sister and me from school to school. Now that he was gone there was no need to pack our raggy bags and move every few months. We stayed put and Mum went to work or brought kids in for minding.

When we were 'on the road', as my father called it, he would get dressed up in silk suits and Indian scarves and things to do his stuff. He called himself The Great Varuna, which, he told us, was the God of Thunder. Sometimes we'd go and watch him perform. I was so proud of him, being able to do things that left other people standing, gaping, wondering, amazed.

I thought my dad was terrific. I didn't stop to think then that it wasn't much of a life for my mum. I didn't realize that she needed him even more than we did. Oh, I knew she cried. We never heard them fight or argue, but when he left the house she would cry and wash her face to hide her tears. But we knew because her eyes would turn blotchy and her face would puff up.

When I was very young, from when I can remember, we moved from town to town, changing houses and schools. Finally, in the last year Dad was with us, we settled down in a flat in Greenford in London. It was only two rooms and a kitchen. My sister and I went to a new school. My dad had a job touring several theatres with a company of performers. His magic act was, at the time, lacking an assistant, because the girl who used to work for him had got fed up of travelling. Dad said she'd found a boyfriend and gone and that she couldn't be replaced because she was worth her weight in gold. She didn't look very heavy to me. Now his act had a rabbit which, during the act, he used to pull out of his big red turban. Dad said it was our job to look after it. The rabbit was called Saffy. It was actually called 'Safaid' which, Dad explained, means 'white' in India – but we called it 'Saffy'.

Mum said we had settled down in Greenford and told us that she wanted us to stay in the same school now that we were six and seven. Dad would spend some nights away and on other nights when he was working near or in London, he would come home after midnight and unpack his stuff and sometimes I would wake up and hear him talking softly to the rabbit as he put him in his cage.

Then, a few months after we got him, poor Saffy got the sniffles. My father, Sonia and I took him to the vet who said he had a sort of rabbit flu and that's why his eyes had got red and his nose was leaking and had begun to get brown and crusty round the edge of the nostrils. She gave us some rabbit pills and asked us if we had any other pets, because he had to be kept away from them or they would get sick too.

That was bad. My father was working then in a small circus. He was supposed to go on tour with it and he wasn't allowed to take Saffy with him because there would be other animals there and the circus manager didn't want a sick and infectious rabbit on their travels.

We were very happy. We'd look after Saffy ourselves while Dad was away. So we kept him in his cage and every evening after school we'd shut the kitchen door and let him out and at weekends we took him down to the common where there were some bushes and let him loose and then spent hours sometimes trying to catch him again, because he used to run away and crouch in hiding places in the foliage.

When my father came back from the circus tour, Saffy seemed much better. We'd take the gunge off his nostrils with cotton wool and hot water every day and apply the cream the vet gave us to his twitching nose. **II**

My mother had been to our school that week and, maybe because she wanted to show off, she told the Headmistress that our dad was a magician and that he would come before the Christmas break and entertain the school for nothing. My father said there was another tour and he had to go back to the circus after a rest, but sure, he'd do a show for our school.

I really wanted him to. Some of the other boys in my school talked about their fathers. Some had shops and sold groceries. Some of them worked for the railway as drivers and ticket collectors. One boy's father was a photographer, but no one's father was anything as intriguing as a magician. The other kids asked me about it, the boys and the girls, and they imagined all sorts of weird things.

'Is your dad haunted?' one kid asked me.

'Does he get his powers from the devil?' another one said.

I said he was just very clever and could make things appear and disappear and now, even those who didn't believe me, would see for themselves. I didn't want to tell them that magic wasn't really magic. That was our secret.

My dad knew I was just waiting for the day of the great performance, when The Great Varuna would bring his magical thunder to our little school stage. Even the teachers began asking me about Dad's magical powers. He was a man of mystery. They hadn't seen him because he never came to the school gates to drop us off or pick us up. He was always on tour or resting from a tour or working in the locked front room, drawing diagrams and making measurements which I thought went into the spells for the new magic.

Then the day of the show arrived and our teacher made us arrange the stage and put out the mats for the children to sit on. I was proud to take charge.

'Will your dad require any chairs on stage or anything?' the teacher asked.

'He said two jugs of water, which he'll bring himself, and a tablecloth for the table. He'll bring that too. He carries everything he needs,' I said.

The one thing I was hoping was that he wouldn't park his big old car in front of the school. It wasn't smart. It was maroon coloured, its bumpers had fallen off and the wheels were all black and dirty. It was funny, but I had never thought about the state of the car before that. It was just Dad's old banger – the magic carpet, he called it.

But he did park the car right in front of the school and he asked the school keeper's assistant to give him a hand with all the stuff he had to carry onto stage.

We were in the playground when he arrived and all the kids went to the fence to watch him come in. He was dressed in his trousers and shirt and he carried his battered old suitcase with its gowns and magician's costumes in it. He waved to me and smiled at the other kids who gathered round him.

'Is that your dad?' they asked.

Some of the bolder kids gathered round him and walked with him asking what the props and stuff were. He was carrying Saffy's cage with a drape over it so no one could see it was a rabbit. He paused and pulled coins out of a boy's nose.

'They didn't come out of his nose,' another kid said.

'You saw it,' my dad said.

'He's snotty and the pounds would be full of snot from his nose,' the cheeky kid said.

After the break we all filed into the hall and sat on the mats.

'Stay away from the radiator cages,' Mr K, our teacher, shouted when some of the kids started rattling the metal cages that were fixed over the central heating radiators in our school hall. The usual disruption was to take a ruler and drag it down stiff over the cage to make a racket, and when ten kids did it at the same time it sounded really horrible.

Then the show started and there was a sudden hush. Dad came on in a blue silk gown with the signs of the Zodiac on it – moons and stars and a few reverse-Swastika signs.

'Is your dad a Nazi?' the kid next to me asked.

'They're not Nazi Swastikas. Those are anticlockwise. These are clockwise and they are ancient Indian signs for good luck,' I said.

It was what my father had told me and I would have thought the other Indian kids in the school, and there were quite a few, would have known that.

He introduced himself as The Great Varuna and told the kids he had to have his lunch and then he started swallowing a long string of coloured scarves knotted together. He must have eaten fifteen of them tied together. The whole school laughed and then Dad opened his mouth and the scarves were gone. Empty mouth. He'd swallowed them.

'You ate them!' a little girl from Year 2 in the front row shouted.

Dad smiled and pulled the scarves out of his mouth one by one. They were not knotted now and he fluttered each of them, as they emerged from his mouth, crisp and dry and ironed. He got a huge clap and I knew I was grinning with pride.

I could see he wanted an even bigger clap and he asked Mr Bulford, the teacher who was standing by the stage, for his watch. The teacher took off his watch and gave it to Dad, who put it on a sheet of metal and smashed it to bits with a big hammer. The kids all gasped and the little girl stood up and shouted, 'That's naughty, that's naughty'.

Dad showed the front row of kids the bits and then he flung them out of an open window.

Bully, which is what we all called Mr Bulford, grinned foolishly.

'Takes the weight off your wrist, doesn't it?' Dad asked him.

'That is a very expensive watch,' Bully said.

'You mean it was a very expensive watch?' Dad said.

The kids didn't know whether to laugh or not because everyone was scared of Bully-boy who was very strict. Dad didn't keep the kids in suspense much longer. He turned to a boy in the front row.

'Now why have you stolen your teacher's watch?' he asked.

The boy looked puzzled.

'Get it out of your pocket,' Dad said and the boy dipped into his pocket and there was the watch. He pulled it out. He couldn't believe his eyes. He gave it back to Bully.

'You must teach them not to steal watches,' Dad said, and everyone clapped loud and long.

Dad did a few more tricks. He gave four kids in the front row sheets of paper and crayons and asked them to draw quick pictures. He took the pictures and held them up and then he shuffled them in front of our eyes, turned them round once and twice and showed us the sheets of paper, and the drawings had disappeared. He handed the sheets round again. There was nothing on them. He asked the same children to do another drawing quickly or write their names in crayon. Then he took the sheets of paper and held them up and when he turned them round the drawings they had first done were back again.

'How weird is that. Your dad's cool, guy,' the boy who had asked about the Nazi sign said.

It was all going too well. Dad picked up the red silk hat and showed it to the audience. It was empty. Then he put his hand in and pulled Saff out of it. The girls all went 'Aww', and the girl in front said, 'Tweet lickle wabbit', and everyone laughed.

But Saffy looked a bit miserable and I could see that the thing on his nostrils had started again because they were dry and scabby. Maybe no one else could see that, but I was thinking Dad should have avoided this trick and done something else. After all he had worked his magic without Saffy for two weeks. He didn't have to bring him along. **II**

Then he made him disappear again. He covered up the hat with a black cloth and put the hat on the table. The cloth jumped up and down, showing that Saffy was still in there dancing about. Then he took the cloth away and the rabbit wasn't in the hat which Dad passed around to show people that it didn't have a false bottom or top or whatever.

'Where did it go?' the girl in the front row said, turning round and looking at the rest of the audience with a raised hand.

And then, just as Dad was stooping to take the hat back, a button or fastening snapped in the fold of his silk gown and the gown fell open. Saffy, white and sniffing now with a faint sound, which sounded very loud in the silent hall, fell out of the gown and scrambled to his feet in the hall. Dad scrambled to shut the flap in his silken gown. Before he did, the audience could see that he had long johns on underneath with pockets and straps and buckles of all sorts. Or perhaps they hadn't noticed that as I had. Perhaps they were looking at the rabbit.

'There he is!' said the little commentating girl.

I'll never forget the startled look on Dad's face. I held my breath. He would pass it off as an intentional joke, part of the magic. How did the rabbit get from the hat to a pouch in his long johns?

But for once my father, The Great Varuna, slipped. He got down and tried to grab Saffy who hopped away from him into the audience. Instead of letting him go, Dad scrambled through the audience after him. The whole hall laughed. And again I saw Dad's eyes. For the first time in my life I saw panic in them. I had never seen panic in anyone's eyes before. **II**

Safir ran into one of the radiator cages and found a gap below one and crawled in.

'The radiators are boiling hot, he'll get roasted,' Mr K shouted and Dad was on his hands and knees groping to grab Saffy from under the cage. I was standing up and desperately watching the magic aura around my father melt away.

Dad struggled to pull Saffy out from under the metal wire of the cage and Saffy struggled to get away. He finally pulled him out and as he did it, the wire cut his forearm and made it bleed. Dad stood up, holding the rabbit and looking confused. Drops of blood began to fall from his forearm and then, in another separate flow, from below Saffy's belly. There was a boy sitting next to the cage and the drops of blood fell on him and he raised his arm and stood up.

'His willy is bleeding. The rabbit's willy,' the boy shouted.

The whole hall went wild. Bully and the headmistress came to the front of the hall, and Dad just stood there holding the bleeding rabbit as though he didn't quite know what had happened. I looked at him and I should never have seen that. It was seeing my father without anything with which to fight the world. It was like seeing him without any clothes on. My heart beat faster and felt as though it was sinking inside me.

It seemed to me that Dad stood like that for a long time, but it may only have been one second. And just like Dad, he tried to make a joke of it.

'No-one escapes The Great Varuna.' he said. 'Don't worry about the blood. It only looks like he's bleeding. Seeing is deceiving.'

He went back and climbed the three steps leading to the stage but the headmistress who had rushed to the front of the hall by then said, 'No, no, Mr Varuna, I can clearly see he really is bleeding. You had better do something. School, quiet! The show's over. Thank you, Mr Varuna. We need to find a bandage for that animal.'

She went up to him and tried to take the bleeding rabbit from his hands but Dad held on to it and pulled Saffy away. The headmistress's hands came away all bloody.

'Leave him to me,' Dad was shouting.

I didn't hear or see any more. I shot out of the hall. The gate was shut and locked but we knew how to get out of school through the hedge and I was out and away. I ran home.

Sonia came back at home time. I couldn't bring myself to tell my mum what had happened at school. I couldn't tell her that I never wanted to go back to that school again. She kept asking me why I had come home, about the show and about Dad, but I wouldn't say a word. I couldn't, Sonia came home and I told her the whole story so she knew all it when Dad came back.

Dad came home after dinnertime. He had been in the pub drinking and the alcohol was on his breath. He tried to act normal and started unloading his equipment from the back of the car and bringing it up the stairs in stages. The last thing he brought up was Saffy in his cage. The cage still had the drape over it.

He went to the kitchen and took out a bottle of brandy he kept there. Mum went in and took it from him. Meanwhile Sonia lifted the drape on Saffy's cage. The white rabbit was crouching in a pool of blood and breathing hard.

'Dad, get the vet. Take him to the vet,' I shouted and both Mum and Dad came out of the kitchen. Mum took one look at Saffy and held her face in horror.

Dad stepped up to the cage, dropped the drape and took the cage into the kitchen.

He shut the kitchen door behind him.

'No, Dad. No, you can't!' I shouted and tried to get into the kitchen but he had bolted it on the other side. He didn't say anything. Both Sonia and I banged on the door until our fists were blue. My mum sat on the sofa, tears down her cheeks.

We heard the taps of the sink turn on in a gush and the pipes in the whole flat began to hum. We carried on pounding the door. I don't know if Sonia knew why we were banging it, but I certainly did.

After a minute or perhaps it was more, my dad unbolted the door and came out of the kitchen with a plastic carrier bag with the limp, long weight in it. He walked out of the front door.

In the kitchen the cage was open on the floor and still bloody. Mum followed us in and started wetting the sponges to clean it up. In the sink there was the bread knife with blood on it.

My dad returned late at night when we were all in bed. We weren't asleep. Sonia and I slept in the front room on the sofa bed when dad was home and Mum and Dad slept in the bedroom.

'I've buried him,' he said to us. 'No magic could save him. That boy was right. He had ripped something under his belly and he was bleeding to death. Sometimes you have to do what seems cruel.'

I wasn't listening to that.

'It was cruel,' I said. 'You are cruel. You should have taken him to the vet.'

'I don't have money for animal operations,' my father said.

'And you are a useless magician,' I said. 'You showed me up.'

My father didn't reply.

'And... and you... you're not magician at all. Not like a real one.'

I shouldn't have said that and I knew I shouldn't have as soon as I had said it. My dad didn't even look in my face. He turned and went into the bedroom and shut the door. For a long time we heard him arguing with my mother, fighting, trying to keep their voices down – as though we couldn't hear.

I didn't see my father for a few days after that. Mum said he was on tour again, but when he came back he said he had found work in Southall in a shoe shop. We never discussed why he had given up magic, or why, after that school show or after what I had said to him, the magic behind his eyes had died.

He didn't last in the shoe shop. They threw him out. He got another job delivering onions in his beat-up car, but then he lost that when the police caught him for drink driving. He started cleaning houses for a living. Then he got another job.

At the time I didn't know that he was going through all these jobs in different places and that he had given up magic. It was only when I was sixteen years old and in my last year at school that Mum told me that Dad, in those last few months he spent with us, had begun training as an orderly in a mental hospital. He had trained and worked for three or four months and one day, as Mum told it, he didn't return from work. When my mum went to the hospital to find him, they said he had been taken ill himself and had volunteered to stay there as a patient and had been admitted.

Sonia and I were not told about any of this. We found out years later that Mum visited him regularly when we were at school and pretended that he was on tour all that time. And then one day they told her that he had run away. The police were called but they didn't find him. Mum kept all this very quiet from us. She just worked and looked after us and didn't let us see her cry. She secretly phoned his family in India but they didn't reply. Finally the letter from India came. He was there and he was going to find his way in the world, it said. I knew she missed him terribly.

His family didn't like her because he had run away with her and come to England to do magic and they didn't think that doing magic as a profession was good enough, she said.

'Of course it's good enough, it's on TV and some of those magicians are famous all round the world and they are millionaires,' I said.

'Your father did an old-fashioned kind of magic. The magicians nowadays use hidden cameras and holograms and all sorts of mind-bending tricks. Your father could never keep up with that. He knew it.'

And when she said that I remember what I said to him the night Saffy died.

'You are a useless magician,' I said.

That sentence had haunted me from the moment I said it. It was untrue, unjust and… and cruel.

The years passed and every day, several times a day, I would imagine him in strange rooms with strange people. Sometimes with another woman, sometimes with other children. And I desperately wanted to know if he ever thought about us. Did he hate me? All of us? I told myself that even if he did, I would find him one day and find out. I could have a job and could be earning some money and could travel in India, which is where I thought he was. If he was still alive.

Only last year I finished school and came to university in Cambridge. And yesterday, yes, just yesterday my friends and I were going home after an afternoon party when we spotted a circus on Midsummer Common. The three friends I was with decided they wanted to see what this Indian circus was like. They persuaded me to go and I went. It would be a laugh.

And there he was. The ringmaster announced him. He was now calling himself Aflatoon The Magic Goon. He came on and bowed and began his first trick to the music of the band, making a tray of teacups rise from the table on its own. He said, 'begi-begi and jill-jillie' and my heart raced and tears came to my eyes. It was Dad.

I waited until the end. I didn't tell my friends what I was doing but I went round the back of the Big Top to the small tents where he was taking his make-up off.

He shut his eyes as I walked into the tent.

'Oh, God,' he said.

'Why didn't you come home?' I asked.

'Is your mother there?' he asked.

'Of course,' I said.

'And she never...'

'No. She never married again or found anyone else.'

'I was afraid,' he said.

'Of us?'

'No. Of having run away.' he said and he got off the stool and hugged me and cried on my shoulder. He said he desperately wanted to come back. Magic.

Farrukh Dhondy: Like Father, Like Son (ed Tony Bradman, 2006)

Ties That Bind Activities

Treasure's Pocket Money

Before Reading

'Treasure' 1

The writer of the article you are going to read gives her teenage daughter the nickname 'Treasure'. When you call someone a 'treasure' it is usually because they have been helpful or kind.

- As a class discuss some of the different tones that could be used for this nickname, for example affectionate, adoring, angry or sarcastic.

After Reading

'Treasure' 2

- With a partner, choose one of the paragraphs where the writer uses the nickname 'Treasure' at least once. Try reading the paragraph using different tones of voice when you come to the word 'Treasure'. Discuss which tone or tones seem to fit best with the way the mother is feeling about her daughter at this point. Find words or phrases in the text that make you think this.

- Working together, practice reading your paragraph. Be prepared to explain to the class why you think the tone or tones you have chosen work best.

- Share your readings and explanations as a class.

———— Your Own Writing ————

What's So Funny?

Part of the humour in this text comes from the mother's suspicion that her daughter is conning her, for example by pretending not to know how much pocket money her friends get.

■ Choose the funniest bit of the text. Share with a partner which you found most amusing. Talk about why you found it funny, for example:

That's just the kind of thing I do. The mother doesn't seem to realise that Treasure's conning her but we do.

Treasure's Reply

■ In a group of three, write a list of the mother's suspicions, for example:

Treasure, you say you don't know how much pocket money your friends get, but I don't believe you, I bet you talk about it all the time but don't tell me because you get more than they do!

■ Imagine you are Treasure. Write one of the following articles:

- a humorous article replying to your mother's suspicions
- a humorous article about pocket money written for teenagers
- a humorous article about pocket money written for parents.

The Birthday Cake

——— Before Reading ———

100-Word Story

- ■ Write a story of exactly 100 words about a grandmother going to a baker's to buy a birthday cake for her husband.

- ■ Form groups of four or five. Read out your stories to each other. When you have listened to the stories discuss the questions that follow.

  - Do the grandmothers in two or more stories have anything in common?
  - Do the stories have anything else in common?
  - Did anyone write a story that surprised you in some way?

- ■ Share your findings as a class and listen to any stories that were surprising.

——— After Reading ———

Your Response

- ■ Think to yourself for a moment about your response to the text. What did it make you think or feel? Share your thoughts with the person sitting next to you.

- ■ As a class discuss the following questions:

  - Was there anything surprising about the story?
  - Did the grandmother in the story behave in the way you would expect?
  - Were there any similarities and differences between the stories you wrote and this one?

Sympathy and Antipathy

> – Sympathy is a feeling of understanding, or agreement, or of pity or sorrow at someone else's distress.
>
> – Antipathy is a feeling of dislike, anger, opposition or disgust towards a person or a thing.

You are going think about how your feelings for Lucia change during the story.

- ■ Work in a group of three. Re-read the story, discussing and agreeing on places where you feel sympathetic towards Lucia, and places where you feel antipathetic towards her.

- ■ You are now going to prepare a group reading of the story as follows.
    - One member of your group will be the sympathetic reader, reading the parts of the story where you have agreed you feel sympathy for the Lucia.
    - One member of your group will be the antipathetic reader, reading the parts of the story where you have agreed you feel antipathy for the Lucia.
    - The third member of the group will read the rest of the story.

- ■ Join another three to make a group of six. Explain which reader is which. Share your readings of the text and discuss any similarities and differences in the points where you decided to change reader.

───── Your Own Writing ─────

Changing Feelings

- ■ Re-write your 100-word story, adding at least two moments when the reader's feelings for the grandmother would change.

- ■ Try out your story on a partner and see if they recognise the moments where you tried to change their feelings.

Just Like Your Father

Before Reading

New Thinking 1

■ On your own, think of at least three things you used to believe when you were younger, but don't believe anymore.

■ Think about one of these old beliefs and what it was that changed your mind. Was it a gradual process, or did something happen that completely changed your point of view?

■ Write a few sentences explaining what you used to believe, what you believe now and what changed your mind. For example:

I used to believe that my mum and dad were always right and knew everything, but now I know they make mistakes too. One day I came home and asked my mum for help with my maths homework and she couldn't do it. She got really impatient and kept saying how it had changed since her day. I suddenly realised that she didn't know everything.

You could use the sentence starters below to help you, if you wish:

- – I used to believe/think/feel...

- – I thought I knew for certain that...

- – Then...which made me realise...

- – The first time I realised....was....

- – Now I believe/think/feel/realise/understand...

■ As a class, share some of your old beliefs and how you came to change your mind about them.

During Reading

'…I was going to graze the ceiling when I stood up.'

- ■ Read as far as '…I was going to graze the ceiling when I stood up.' **II**

Jacqueline Wilson is well-known for writing about some of the awkward things about being a teenager when you feel part-child part-adult. Josh has always been close to his mum, but as he is growing up he also recognises that he has to make a life separate from her.

- ■ Draw a chart like the one below to trace Josh's conflicting thoughts and feelings about his mum in the section you have read so far.

Quotation showing Josh and his mum are close	Quotation showing Josh growing apart from his mum

'… so he turned into a handsome prince.'

- ■ Read up to '… so he turned into a handsome prince.' **II**

- ■ Work in a group of three. Each of you should take one of the following statements and find evidence to support it in the text.

Josh's dad was a terrible dad.	1

Josh only knows what his mum has told him about his dad.	2

Josh would like to know more about his dad.	3

Josh is worried that he might turn into his dad.	4

Josh thinks it might have been his fault that his dad left.	5

"Kids," he said."

■ Read up to "Kids," he said.' **II**

The advice often given to writers is to 'show not tell' in creative writing. Rather than writing 'this man was obviously a good father' (telling) Jacqueline Wilson shows how he behaves and lets the readers draw their own conclusions (showing).

■ What clues does Jacqueline Wilson give about what kind of dad or grandad this man is? Try to find one sentence, one phrase and one word that give clues. You could use the sentence starters from the 'Before Reading' activity (page 119) to help you, if you wish.

———— After Reading ————

New Thinking 2

■ Think to yourself for a moment about your response to the text. What did it make you think or feel? Share your thoughts with the person sitting next to you.

■ As a class, discuss how Josh has changed by the end of the story. Try to find at least three ways in which he has changed his thinking and find the section of the text that made you think this.

■ Write a paragraph or two in role as Josh, explaining what you used to believe, what you believe now and what changed your mind.

———— Your Own Writing ————

New Thinking 3

■ Write a short piece about Josh's early childhood from the point of view of either his mum, or, if you want to give yourself more of a challenge, his dad.

Begi-begi and Jill-jillie

─── Before Reading ───

Magic 1

What is the best magic trick you've ever seen?

- ■ Think to yourself for one minute.

- ■ Share with your partner.

- ■ Share as a class.

─── During Reading ───

'…apply the cream the vet gave us to his twitching nose.'

- ■ Read as far as '…apply the cream the vet gave us to his twitching nose.' **II**

- ■ With a partner discuss your first impressions of the narrator's father. Do you think he is a good father? Why or why not?

'He didn't have to bring him along.'

- ■ Read as far as 'He didn't have to bring him along.' **II**

- ■ As a class, discuss how you think the audience will react if the narrator's dad gets a trick wrong. Why do you think this?

'I had never seen panic in anyone's eyes before.'

- ■ Read as far as 'I had never seen panic in anyone's eyes before.' **II**

- ■ With a partner, look back through this section. Find as many clues as you can which hinted that there would be a riot if anything went wrong during the magic show.

- ■ As a class, discuss why you think Dhondy put in these clues.

'He said he desperately wanted to come back. Magic.'

- ■ Read to the end of the story.

- ■ With a partner, discuss whether you find the happy ending believable, for example whether it seems to fit with what you have learnt about the characters in the rest of the story.

- ■ Share your idea as a class.

After Reading

Magic 2

◼ With a partner or in a small group, look at the extracts from the text below.

> He had left us, but secretly, without ever saying it to Mum or to Sonia, I felt, as if by magic, he was with us.

> You see Dad was a magician. A real one. But he was strange because he said he didn't believe in magic.

> So that was the spell I used at night, kneeling by my bed and praying to the powers that made magic work, to try and get him back.

> I said he was just very clever and now, even those who didn't believe me, would see for themselves. I didn't want to tell them that magic wasn't really magic. That was our secret.

> I was standing up and desperately watching the magic aura around my father melt away.

> And...and you...you're not a magician at all. Not like a real one.

> ...the magic behind his eyes had died.

> He said he desperately wanted to come back. Magic.

◼ Discuss why you think the idea of magic runs right through the story right up until the last word, 'magic'. Use the prompts below to get you started.

- The theme of magic shows how the father is crushed when his son no longer believes he is a great magician.

- The real magic in the story is in the relationship between father and son which survives despite everything.

Story Structure

The diagrams below could illustrate the way the story is structured.

- With a partner discuss what each diagram is trying to show about the story.

- Discuss which one you think best fits the story and why.

- With your partner, draw the diagram you have chosen and annotate it with quotations and events from the story to show how it fits the diagram.

- Share your thoughts as a class.

1.

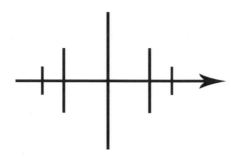

2.

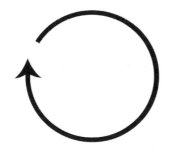

3.

Extension Work

Your Own Writing

- Next time you write a story, try to use one of these story shapes to help you to think about the structure.

Working with More than One Text

'Just Like Your Father' by Jacqueline Wilson and 'Begi-begi and Jill-jillie' by Farrukh Dhondy

For this work you will need to have read 'Just Like Your Father' by Jacqueline Wilson and 'Begi-begi and Jill-jillie' by Farrukh Dhondy.

 **Your Own Writing**

A Father's Letter

Included on page 126 is a letter written by a father after reading Jacqueline Wilson and Farrukh Dhondy's stories.

- Read the letter.

- Half the class should reply to the letter in role as Jacqueline Wilson and half the class in role as Farrukh Dhondy, explaining why you presented the father in the way you did in your story. In your reply you should think about:

  - what you were trying to say about fatherhood
  - whether the way the character was written made the story more interesting than writing about an ideal father
  - who your story is aimed at (children, not parents) and what difference this made to the way you wrote the story
  - whether you think the father in the letter has a point
  - whether you think it is the responsibility of a writer to think about representing particular groups of people fairly.

- Read out some of the replies and decide which sounds most like it was written by Wilson and which sounds most like it was written by Dhondy.

Extension Work

A Good Dad

- Read the letter from a 'good dad' in the 'A Father's Letter' activity above.

- Write a story you think the 'good dad' would like to read.

Dear Jacqueline Wilson and Farrukh Dhondy,

I recently read your stories, 'Just Like Your Father' and 'Begi-begi and Jill-jillie'. I have to say that they are both well-written but I couldn't enjoy them because I'm sick and tired of fathers in stories always being the bad guys. I'm a dad myself and I hope I am a good one. Not perfect of course, but nothing like the fathers I read about in stories and novels.

In the past dads were expected to earn enough money to support their families and to be the disciplinarian if the children misbehaved. That was it. Nowadays they are still expected to do these things but they also have to be able to talk and listen to their children, be caring, loving and reliable. They should work hard to earn lots of money so that their children can have the latest toys, computers, designer clothes or holidays abroad but also be around to play with them and take them to interesting places. I try to do all these things with my children but every time I read another story about a bad dad I feel as if society does not appreciate what a tough job it is to be a good father.

There are plenty of stories about good mothers, as well as bad ones, so why can't you write a story about a good father for a change?

I look forward with interest to your reply,

Yours sincerely,

A good dad

Seeing Things

My Polish Teacher's Tie

Seeing Things in the Dark

One Woman's Cup of Tea

I can't forget the girl in the orange dress

Note to Sixth Grade Self

Note to Sixth-Grade Self

On Wednesdays wear a skirt. A skirt is better for dancing. After school, remember not to take the bus. Go to McDonald's instead. Order the fries. Don't even bother trying to sit with Patricia and Cara. Instead, try to sit with Sasha and Toni Sue. If they won't let you, try to sit with Andrea Shaw. And if Andrea Shaw gets up and throws away the rest of her fries rather than sit with you, sit alone and do not look at anyone. Particularly not the boys. If you do not look at them, they may not notice you sitting alone. And if they don't notice you sitting alone, there is still a chance that one of them will ask you to dance.

At three-thirty stand outside with the others and take the number seven bus uptown. Get off when they all get off. Be sure to do this. Do not stare out the window and lose yourself. You will end up riding out to the edge of town past the rusted gas-storage tanks, and you will never find the right bus home. Pay attention. Do not let the strap of your training bra slip out the armhole of your short-sleeved shirt. Do not leave your bag on the bus. As you cross the street, take a look at the public high school. The kids there will be eating long sticks of Roman candy and leaning on the chain-link fence. Do they look as if they care who dances with whom, or what steps you'll learn this week? News flash: They do not. Try to understand that there's a world larger than the one you inhabit. If you understand that, you will be far ahead of Patricia and Cara.

For now, though, you live in this world, so go ahead and follow the others across the street to Miggie's Academy of Dance. There is a low fence outside. Do not climb on it in your skirt. Huddle near the door with the other girls. See if anyone will let you listen. Do not call attention to yourself. Listen as Patricia, with her fascinating stutter, describes what she and Cara bought at the mall. Notice how the other girls lean forward as she works through her troublesome consonants: *G-G-Guess Jeans and an Esp-p-prit sweater.* They will talk about the TV shows they watch, who killed whom, who is sleeping with whom; they will compare starlets' hairstyles. None of this talk is of any importance. For God's sake, don't bother watching those TV shows. Keep reading your books.

At four o'clock, go inside with the others. Line up against the wall with the girls. Watch how the boys line up against their wall, popular ones in the middle, awkward ones at the sides. Watch how the girls jockey to stand across from the boys they like.

Watch Brittney Wells fumble with the zipper of her nylon LeSportsac. Don't let her get next to you with that thing. Try to stand across from someone good. Do not let yourself get pushed all the way out to the sides, across from Zachary Booth or Ben Dusseldorf. Watch how Patricia and Cara stand, their hips shot to one side, their arms crossed over their chests. Try shooting your hip a little to one side. Rest your weight on one foot. Draw a circle on the wooden floor with one toe. Do not bite your fingernails. Do not give a loud sniff. Think of the word *nonchalant*. Imagine the eleventh-graders, the way they look when they smoke on the bus. Let your eyes close halfway.

When Miss Miggie comes out, do not look at her enormous breasts. Breasts like those will never grow on your scarecrow body. Do not waste your time wanting them. Instead, watch how she moves in her low-cut green dress: chin high, back straight, hips asway. Listen to the way she talks: Fawx Trawt, Chaw-chaw, Wawtz. Love how she talks, but do not pick it up. When you move north in three years, you cannot afford to say *y'all*. Listen as Miss Miggie describes what y'all will learn that day. Watch how her hand traces the dance steps in the air. Now that the boys are occupied, staring at her breasts, you can look openly at Eric Cassio. Admire his hair and eyes, but quickly. Like all boys he will feel you looking.

The first dance will always be a cha-cha. On the record they will sing in Spanish, a woman trilling in the background. It will start a thrill in your chest that will make you want to move. Watch Miss Miggie demonstrate the steps. Practice the steps in your little rectangle of floor. Watch how Patricia and Cara do the steps, their eyes steady in front of them, their arms poised as if they were already holding their partners. Now concentrate on dancing. Avoid Sasha and Toni Sue with their clumsy soccer-field legs. Ignore Brittney and that purse. When Miss Miggie looks at you, concentrate hard. Remember practicing with your father. Do not throw in an extra dance step that you are not supposed to know yet. Do not swish your skirt on purpose. Do not look at the boys. ❙❙

Long before it is time to pick partners, you will feel the tightness in your stomach. Do not let it break your concentration. You have too many things to learn. Remember, if you want to have the most gold stars at the end of the eight weeks, you are going to have to work hard. Imagine dancing in a spotlight at the end-of-class ball, with the best boy dancer from all the seven private schools. On the Achievement Record, next to your name, there are already five stars. Patricia and Cara also have five stars. Everyone else has two or three. Think of the stars in their plastic box. You can almost taste the adhesive on their backs. Two more stars can be yours today, if you do not let yourself get nervous.

When it is time for the boys to pick, do not bite your hangnails. Do not pull at your skirt. Watch how Patricia and Cara lean together and whisper and laugh, as if they don't care whether or not they get picked. Watch how Miss Miggie brings her arms together, like a parting of the Red Sea in reverse, to start the picking. The boys will push off with their shoulder blades and make their way across the floor. Do not make eye contact! If you make eye contact you will drown. Do not, whatever you do, look at Eric Cassio. You do not care which one of those other girls he picks. You know it will not be you.

When the picking is over, hold your chin up and wait for Miss Miggie to notice you standing alone. She will take Zachary Booth by the shoulder and steer him over to you. When he is standing in front of you, look down at his white knee socks. Stand silent as he asks, with his lisp, if he can have thith danth. Ignore the snorts and whispers of your classmates. Do not think about Zachary Booth's hand warts. Let him take your right hand and put his left hand stiffly at your waist. Be glad you are dancing with a boy at all, and not with Brittney Wells, as you did last week.

When Miss Miggie starts the music, raise your chin and look Zachary Booth in the eye. Make sure he knows that even though he is the boy, you will be the one to lead. As much as he hates to dance with you, he will be grateful for that. It will be up to you alone to make sure you don't both look like fools. Squeeze his hand when it is time to start. Whisper the steps under your breath. When he falters, keep right on going. Let him fall back in step with you. Out of the corner of your eye, watch Miss Miggie drifting through the room as she claps the rhythm, her red mouth forming the words *one two*. When she looks your way, remember your father's advice: head high, shoulders back. Smile at Zachary Booth. Ignore the grimace he makes in return. If you dance well you may be picked to demonstrate.

And you know which boy will be picked. You know who is picked to demonstrate nearly every time, who Miss Miggie always *wants* to pick, even when she has to pick one of the others just to mix things up. Eric Cassio is not just great in *your* opinion. Already the world understands how excellent he is. The music swells toward its final cha-cha-cha and Miss Miggie's eyes scan the room. Her red lips come together like a bow. She raises her rack of breasts proudly and lifts her finger to point. The finger flies through the air toward Eric Cassio, and Miss Miggie calls his name. He scowls and looks down, pretending to be embarrassed, but there is a smile at the corner of his mouth. Patricia bites a fingernail. Understand that she is nervous. This gives you power. Do not flinch when Zachary Booth pinches your arm; do not let the burning in your eyes become tears. He does not concern you. The only thing that concerns you is who Miss Miggie will point to next. It could be anyone. It could be you. Her finger flies through the air. Is it you? Oh, God, it is.

Do not look at Patricia and Cara as they extend their tongues at you. Ignore Zachary Booth's explicit hand gesture. Forget you weigh sixty-nine pounds; stop wanting breasts so badly. So what if you wear glasses? So what if your skirt is not Calvin Klein? For this one moment you have no hangnails, no bony knees, and there is a secret between you and Eric Cassio. When the others clear the floor, look him square in the eye and share that secret. The secret is, you know he likes to dance. It goes back to the day when you were punished together for being tardy[1], when you had to transplant all the hybrid peas from the small white plastic pots to the big terracotta ones. Your hands touched, down in the bag of potting soil. When you got cold he gave you his green sweater. Later, as you were cleaning up – the water was running, no one could hear him – he told you he *liked* to dance. Remember these things. The fact that he ignored you at lunch that day, at recess, and every day afterward – even the fact that he is now Patricia's boyfriend – does not matter. He *likes* to dance. Look into his eyes, and he will remember he told you.

Let his arm come around you, tanned and slim. Take his hand; it is free of warts. The dance requires that you maintain eye contact with him almost constantly. Do not be afraid to meet his blue eyes. Smile. Remember what your father has taught you: Cuban motion. It is in the hips. A white boat rocking on waves. The half-hour demonstration with your mother, her hair upswept, was not for nothing. Here you are. Miss Miggie lowers the arm onto the record, and the maracas shake into action.

When you dance with Eric Cassio, communicate through your hands. A press here, a sharp squeeze there, and you'll know what he wants you to do, and he'll know what you want him to do. As you change directions, catch Patricia's eye for one moment. Give your hips the Cuban motion. Make her watch. When you twirl, twirl sharp. Listen to Miss Miggie clapping in rhythm. Let all the misery fall out of your chest. Smile at Eric. He will smile back, just with the corner of his mouth. He is remembering transplanting the peas. He does not smile at Patricia that way; that is a smile for you.

Do the special pretzel thing with your arms, that thing Miss Miggie has only shown you once; pull it off without a hitch. End with your back arched and your leg outstretched. Listen to the silence that comes over the room like fog. Remember the way they look at you. No one will applaud. Five seconds later, they will hate you more than ever.

The next day, watch out. You will pay for that moment with Eric. Wear pants, for God's sake. Take no chances. In gym you will play field hockey; remember that this is not one of your better games. You are on the red team, Patricia and Cara are on the blue. You are left wing forward. When you get the ball, pass it as quickly as you can. What will happen is inevitable, but it will be worse if you make them mad. It will happen at the end of the game, when you are tired and ready for gym to be over. As you race down the side of the field toward the ball, halfback Cara's stick will come out and trip you. You will fall and sprain your wrist. Your glasses will fly off and be broken in two at the nosepiece. You will cut your chin on a rock.

[1] *Tardy = late*

131

Lie still for a moment in the trampled clover. Try not to cry. The game will continue around you as if you do not exist. Only the gym teacher, leathery-skinned Miss Schiller, will notice that anything is wrong. She will pick you up by the arm and limp you over to the bench. Do not expect anyone to ask if you are okay. If they cared whether or not you were okay, this would never have happened. Let this be a lesson to you about them. When Patricia scores a goal they cluster around her, cheering, and click their sticks in the air.

At home, seek medical assistance. Do not let anything heal improperly. You will need that body later. As your mother binds your wrist in an Ace bandage, you will tell her you tripped on a rock. She will look at you askance. Through instinct, she will begin to understand the magnitude of your problem. When she is finished bandaging you, she will let you go to your room and be alone with your books. Read the final chapters of *A Little Princess*. Make an epic picture of a scene from a girls' boarding school in London on three sheets of paper. Push your brother around the living room in a laundry basket. That night, in the bath, replay in your head the final moment of your dance with Eric Cassio. Ignore the fact that he would not look at you that day. Relish the sting of bathwater on your cuts. Tell yourself that the moment with Eric was worth it. Twenty years later, you will still think so.

That weekend something will happen that will seem like a miracle: Patricia will call you on the phone. She will tell you Cara's sorry for tripping you in gym. Look down at your purple swollen wrist, touch the taped-together bridge of your glasses. Say it's no big deal. Patricia will ask what you are doing that afternoon. You will whisper, 'Nothing.' She will ask you to meet her and Cara at Uptown Square.

– We're going shopping for d-d-dresses for the Miggie's B-ball, she'll say. Wanna come?

Now, think. *Think.* Do you really believe Cara could be sorry, that suddenly she and Patricia could crave your company? And even if they did, would you want these girls as friends? Try to remember who you're dealing with here. Try to tell Patricia you will not go shopping.

Of course, you will not refuse. You will arrange a time and place to meet. Then you will spend half an hour picking out an outfit, red Chinese-print pants and a black shirt, matching shoes and earrings. You will ask your mother to drive you to the mall, and she will consent, surprise and relief plain on her face. She will even give you her credit card.

When you arrive at the entrance to Uptown Square, with its marble arches and potted palms, you will pretend to see Patricia and Cara inside. You will kiss your mother and watch her drive away. Then you will stand beside the potted palms and wait for Patricia and Cara. You will take off your broken glasses and put them in your pocket, and adjust the hem of your shirt. You will wait there for ten minutes, fifteen, twenty. When you run inside to use the bathroom you will hurry your way through, afraid that you're keeping them waiting, but when you go outside again they will still not be there.

You will wonder whether Patricia meant *next* week. You will bite your nails down to the quick, then continue biting.

Stop this. They are not coming.

Go inside. Wander toward the fountain with the alabaster naked ladies. Sit down at the fountain's edge and look at the wavering copper and silver circles beneath the water. Don't waste time thinking about drowning yourself. Don't bother imagining your funeral, with your classmates in black clothes on a treeless stretch of lawn. If you die you will not be there to see it, and your classmates probably won't be either.

Instead, take a nickel from your pocket and make your own wish: Patricia and Cara strung upside-down from the tree in the schoolyard, naked for all the world to see. Kiss your nickel and toss it in. Feel better. Dry your eyes. Here you are in Uptown Square with your mother's credit card. Go to Maison Blanche, past the children's department, straight to Preteens. Tell the glossy-haired woman what kind of dress you want: something short, with a swirly skirt. Look through all the dresses she brings you; reject the ones with lace and flounces. On your own, look through all the others on the rack. You will almost give up. Then, at the very back, you will find your dress. It is midnight-blue with a velvet spaghetti-strap bodice and a satin skirt. Tell yourself it is the color of Eric Cassio's eyes. Try it on. Watch it fit. Imagine yourself, for a moment, as a teenager, an eleventh-grader, the girls you see in the upper school bathroom brushing their hair upside down and flipping it back. Flip your hair back. Twirl in front of the mirror. The dress costs fifty-eight dollars, with tax. Pay with your mother's credit card. The woman will wrap it in white tissue and seal it with a gold sticker, then slide it into a white store bag. By the time your mother comes to pick you up, you'll have almost forgotten about Patricia and Cara. When she asks you how your afternoon went, lie. **▌▌**

School this next week will be hell. Everyone will know about Patricia and Cara's trick on you, how you went to the mall and waited. Now you will have to pay a price. People will come up to you all day and ask you to their birthday parties and family picnics and country clubs. Do not dignify them with a response, particularly not crying. This will be extremely difficult, of course. Try to understand what's going on: You got to dance with Eric Cassio, and he refused to act as if you made him sick. This is a threat to the social order.

By Tuesday afternoon, things will become unbearable. It is a dull week – preparations for a spring pageant, the history of the Louisiana Purchase, sentence diagramming in Language Arts – and people have nothing better to talk about. After lunch, on the playground, they gather around you as you try to swing. They needle you with questions: How many hours did you wait? Did you cry? Did you make believe you had a pretend friend? Did you have to call your mommy?

Get out of the swing. Be careful. You are angry. Words do not come easily around your classmates, particularly not at times like these. But you cannot let them continue to think that they have made you miserable. Tell them you went to Maison Blanche and bought a blue velvet dress.

– Liar! You can't afford a dress from Maison Blanche.

– I did.

– No, you d-didn't. I think you bought a d-d-d-

– A *diaper*, Cara finishes.

– It's a blue velvet dress. With spaghetti straps.

– They don't even h-h-h-have a dress like that there. You n-never went in there, you liar. You were too b-busy crying. *Waah-aah!* No one likes me! You bought a d-d-d-d-dirty baby diaper. You're wearing it right now! Ew, ew.

Ew, ew, ew. They run away from you, holding their noses, and tell their friends you had to wear a diaper because you kept stinking up your pants. Back in the classroom, before the teacher gets back, they push their desks into a tight little knot on the other side of the room. Finally you understand the vocabulary word *ostracize*. Look away from them. Stare at the blackboard. Swallow. Out of the corner of your eye, glance at Eric Cassio. He will be watching you, not laughing with the others. Patricia will lean over and whisper in his ear, and he will answer her. But he will not – not once – laugh at your expense.

When the teacher comes in and asks what on earth is going on, everyone will start moving the desks back without a word. Soon you will all get lost in the angles and word shelves of a sentence diagram. After that, Math. Then the bus ride home. Now you can spend all evening sulking in the alcove of your bedroom. When your parents come to tell you it's time for dinner, you will tell them you have a headache. You will cry and ask for orange children's aspirin. Half an hour later your little brother will come to you with a plate of food, and he will sit there, serious-eyed, as you eat it.

Later that night you will hear your parents in their bedroom, talking about sending you to a different school. Your father is the champion of this idea. When your mother argues that things might be getting better for you, you will secretly take her side. You tell yourself that leaving the school would mean giving up, letting the others win. You will not have that. You will not go to the schools your father suggests: Newman, your rival, or Lakeside, a religious day school. You will get angry at him for mentioning it. Doesn't he believe you can prove yourself to them, get friends, even become popular?

You blind, proud, stupid, poor dunce. ▌▌

Next day, you will take the dress to school. Why, for God's sake? Why? Won't they see it at the Miggie's Ball anyway? But you insist on proving to them that it's real, despite the obvious danger. You will carry it in the Maison Blanche bag to show you really bought it there. When it's time for morning recess, you will casually take the bag out of your locker as if you have to move it to put some books away. Patricia and Cara will stop at your locker on their way out. You will pretend not to see them. Notice, however, that Eric Cassio is standing in the doorway waiting for them.

– Look, she b-brought a bag of baby d-d-d-d-

– You're stinking up the whole place, Cara says.

You pick up the bag so that the tissue inside crinkles, then steal a glance inside and smile to yourself.

– Is that your K-mart dress for the Miggie's Ball?

– Can I b-borrow it? Patricia takes the bag from you and holds it open. You feel a flash of fear, seeing it in her hands. Look at Eric Cassio. He is staring at his shoes. Patricia takes out the tissue-wrapped dress and tears the gold sticker you have kept carefully intact. As she shakes it out and holds it against herself, she and Cara laugh.

– Look at me. I'm Cinderella. I'm Cher.

Tell her to give it back.

– Oh, sure. C-come and g-get it. Patricia lofts the dress over your head in a blur of blue; Cara catches it.

– Don't you want it, stinky baby? Cara shakes it in your face, then throws it over your head again to Patricia.

Patricia holds the dress over your head. She is three inches taller than you. You jump and catch the hem in one hand and hold on tight. When Patricia pulls, you pull too. Finally she gives a sharp yank. There is a terrible sound, the sound of satin shearing, detaching itself from velvet. Patricia stumbles back with half your dress in her hands. Her mouth hangs open in a perfect O. Outside, kids shriek and laugh at recess. A kickball smacks against the classroom wall.

Cara will be the first to recover. She will take the half-dress from Patricia and shrug.

– Oh, well, she says. It was just an ugly dress.

– Yeah, Patricia says, her voice flat and dry. And a stupid b-brand.

Cara will throw the piece of dress at you. Let it fall at your feet. Suppress the wail of rage inside your rib cage. Do not look at Eric Cassio. Do not move or speak. Wait for them to leave. When the classroom door closes behind them, sit on the floor and stuff the rags of your dress back into the paper bag. Stare at the floor tile, black grains swirling into white. See if you can make it through the next five minutes. The next ten. Eventually, you'll hear the class coming back from recess. Get to your feet and dust off your legs. Sit down at your desk and hold the bag in your lap.

You will remember a story you heard on the news, about a brother and sister in Burma who got caught in a flood. As they watched from a rooftop, the flood stripped their house of its walls, drowned their parents against a bamboo fence, and washed their goats and chickens down the road. Their house is gone. Their family is gone. But they hold on to a piece of wood and kick toward dry land. Think how they must have felt that night, kicking into the flood, the houses all around them in splinters, people and animals dead. **❚❚**

On Saturday, wear something good: a pair of white shorts and a red halter and sandals. Put your hair in a barrette. Try not to think about the dress in its bag at the bottom of your closet. That does not concern you. Go downstairs and get something to eat. You will not erase yourself by forgoing meals. After breakfast, when your mother asks if you'd like to make cookies, say yes. Look how much this pleases her. You have not felt like doing anything in weeks. Take out the measuring cups and bowls and all the ingredients. Mix the dough. Allow your brother to add the chocolate chips.

Put the cookies in the oven. Check them at three minutes, and at five. Your brother claps his hands and asks again and again if they are ready yet. When they are ready, open the oven door. A wash of sugary heat will hit your face. Pull on the mitts and take out the cookie sheet. Just then, the doorbell will ring.

Listen as your mother gets the door. You will hear her talking to someone outside, low. Then she'll come into the kitchen.

– There's a boy here for you, she says, twisting her hands in her apron. He wants to ride bikes.

– Who?

– I don't know. He's blond.

Do not drop the tray of cookies on the kitchen tile. Do not allow your head to float away from your body. The familiar tightness will gather in your throat. At first you will think it is another joke, that when you go to the door he will not be there.

But then there he is, in the doorway of the kitchen. It is the first time in years someone else your age has stood inside your house. And this is Eric Cassio, in his blue-striped Oxford shirt and khaki shorts, his hair wild from the wind. Watch him stare at your brother, who's gotten a handful of cookie dough. Try talking. Offer him some cookies and milk. Your mother will take your brother, silently, out into the yard, and in a few moments you will hear him shrieking as he leaps through the sprinkler.

Now eat a cookie and drink milk with Eric Cassio. Do not let crumbs cling to your red halter. Wipe the line of milk from your upper lip. Watch Eric eat one cookie, then another. When he's finished he will take a rumpled white package from his backpack and push it across the table. You will be extremely skeptical. You will look at the package as if it were a bomb.

– I told my mom what happened at school, he says. She got you this.

Turn the package over. It is a clothing bag. When you open it you will find a dress inside, a different one, dark red with a jewel neckline and two small rosettes at the hip.

– I know it's not the same as the other one, he says.

Look at him, hard, to make sure this is not a joke. His eyes are steady and clear. Stand up and hold the dress up against you. You can see it is just the right size. Bite your lip. Look at Eric Cassio, speechless. Try to smile instead; he will understand.

– Patricia won the Miggie's thing, he says. She told me last night.

For a moment, you will feel bludgeoned. You thought it would be you. You and Eric Cassio. It was supposed to make all the difference. Patricia couldn't possibly have more stars than you. Then remember there's another important thing to ask him.

– Who's the boy?

He looks down into his lap, and you understand that the boy is him. When he raises his eyes, his expression tells you that despite the dress, despite the hybrid peas, things are not going to change at school or at Miss Miggie's. He will not take walks with you at recess or sit next to you at McDonald's. You can see he is apologizing for this, and you can choose to accept or not.

Get to your feet and pull yourself up straight; raise your chin as your mother has shown you to do. Adjust the straps of your sandals, and make sure your halter is tied tight. Then ride bikes with Eric Cassio until dark.

Julie Orringer: How to Breathe Underwater (2005)

Seeing Things in the Dark

Lucinda Roy, a writer and lecturer, tells the story of the year she spent as a volunteer teacher in Sierra Leone. Background information on Sierra Leone is given on page 156.

When I went to Africa for two years as a volunteer teacher, I was twenty-one. I was afraid, not of the land itself, but of being without my mother, my best friend. How would I manage to find happiness thousands of miles from her laughter? I was a girl alone, hardly a woman yet. How would I be able to uncover places in the land that knew me? I'd never travelled outside of Europe before. I didn't know the local language. I was afraid of puff adders and malaria, leprosy and crocodiles. Most of all, I was afraid that the people would not like me. For a 'coloured girl' raised in London, Africa meant going home to my ancestors, but home had been England for twenty-one years. If no one recognized me in Sierra Leone, how would I recognize myself?

Two and a half decades later, having lived now on three continents, I am accustomed to abiding within my own difference. With my Jamaican and British heritage, I am not your typical Brit anyway. And there is something sweet about singularity – something that says I will never have to see the same things others see. But back then, yearning for the familiar stole my breath away and almost made me forget to see that I was being blessed.

It was pouring when I first set foot in Sierra Leone. The heat was like a swaddling cloth, and the darts of rain met the ground as steam. I travelled in the back of a van to the Catholic girls' school in Lunsar where I would be teaching. I sat in the windowless back of the vehicle with a young Sierra Leonean of about eleven who had needed a ride to and from the capital city. Every time the priest who was driving swerved to avoid a pothole, the boy would murmur in terror. I tried to comfort him, but we didn't speak each other's language; even if we had, his terror was beyond words. So great was it, in fact, that it eclipsed my own for a while. Fear didn't surface again until we pulled up to the concrete block, single-story house I would occupy for the next two years. In my bedroom was a bed, a table, and a chair. Outside, the rain came down and hit the tin roof like the wrath of Jehovah. When night came I sprayed the room with Shelltox to kill anything living within ten feet of me, checked my slippers for tarantulas, tucked in the mosquito net around the wafer thin mattress in a ritual that bordered on paranoia, and listened to the sound of drums coming through the bush. I didn't just taste fear, I feasted on it. Why had I travelled so far? Home, though times had been hard, was more comfortable than this. I wanted a burger. I wanted a television. I wanted to be someone's daughter again.

Each day I walked down the pink dust road to Our Lady of Guadalupe to teach English to girls who came from regions throughout the country and who were taught by the nuns to behave like someone's idea of a 'lady.' Each day two hundred voices rang out across the playing field as the girls spoke Temne, Mende, Krio, and English, and I sat in the teacher's lounge, wishing for a fan, just one fan, to mitigate the heat. Each morning I found a large mound of ants and soil in the corner of my living room where I had swept the night before, and each evening when I went into the kitchen, a dozen roaches scurried away to hide in the dark. My anger was often directed at the nuns and the priests, many of whom lived as strangers among the people, importing wine and cheese from Italy, and speaking with certainty about truth and redemption. Yet I too lived as a stranger among the local people, waiting for the next food package from my mother, or the next trip to the capital so that I could buy real ketchup and mayonnaise.

At twenty-one I became a teacher of young women who looked at me with hunger, and who dreamed of wearing watches and contact lenses, of travelling to England and America, and of working in the city at a bank or a hotel. A group of Namibian girls, brought to the school by missionaries from the south, sat in the shade during study periods and sang about their families and home. The father of one of them had been hanged for insurrection and the others didn't know how many of their relatives had been killed in the war. Their voices threaded inside of one another until their harmony was as tight as the braids on their heads, and no individual voice could be picked out from the entwined grieving tones. They brought out in me an even deeper yearning for those I'd left behind in England – a yearning I felt guilty about. After all my dreams of making a difference, I had arrived in West Africa with too much baggage to be any good to anyone.

For several months I closed my eyes. I refused to see the beauty of the women as they balanced firewood or huge bowls of water on their heads. I couldn't see the sweetness on the faces of my neighbours' children. I forgot to look at the way the bananas on the tree in my backyard were turning from green to gold. City life had pulled a veil over my eyes. Like many travellers who forget to surrender to the journey, what I saw was a country that occupied the negative space of my vision. In the foreground was London and the familiar roar of urban life. I lived in West Africa, but I wasn't really there. I talked with other volunteers: Peace Corps volunteers from America and CUSO volunteers from Canada. Because they remembered what I had known, we would reminisce like elderly people who have seen the best of times once and want to return to them again.

Then one day I went to collect the mail as usual. The journey to the post office was quicker if I cut through the bush. I greeted the woman who sold sweet potato sandwiches and the man who was stoking his fire ready for meat sticks laced with red hot peppers. '*Kusheh*[1],' we said to each other. '*Kusheh-ya*.' But my greeting was hollow. I had tunnel vision. At the end of the tunnel was a letter from home. The bush ran past me like a scared animal. The blue airmail envelope was the prize I had to have.

At the post office the grey metal mailboxes that lined one side of an outside wall glinted in the glare of the tropical sun. I opened my box with my precious key. Nothing. No letters from home. Although my mother wrote to me every other day, it wasn't enough. I was self-pitying to the point of fury. I turned around to walk back through the bush and almost stepped into the body of a boy. I jerked backward and felt the warm metal mailboxes on my spine.

The boy was closer to me than my shadow. His face was that of an old man, and his eyes were lined with what once must have been expectation but which had now been replaced by a kind of bitterness. He shoved something toward me and I leaped out of the way, backing off as I spoke. It took me a while to realize that what he was trying to shove in my face was his arm. I hadn't recognized it at first because so much of it had been eaten away. Raw pink flesh and yellow pus were having a kind of party on his forearm. In Krio, he demanded money, forced me to look again at his pitiful limb. In his tone was the anger of the poor and the dispossessed. I'd had it in my voice as a child when I had to call out in class, 'Yes, I am a free lunch person.' I recognized it. It made me sick.

I would like to tell you that I took him in my arms and carried him to the mission hospital to be healed, though the wound looked strangely aged, as though the boy had lived with his suffering for months. But it would be a lie. Instead, a terrible thought came to me before I could censor it. I thought: The colours on his arm clash with each other. And then I backed away because, in spite of my colour, I was from the West, and fear was a noose around my neck.

It was only later, when I dared to let myself think of what had happened, that I felt an overwhelming sense of shame. Deeper than the fear that had held me in its grip for

[1] *Kusheh = Hello in Krio*

140

months, shame took hold like fire can and made me journey back to the post office for weeks afterward, looking for the child I had turned away. I never found him. But there were others who took his place.

Little by little, the British fog began to rise. I don't recall when it was that I first noticed the haunting beauty in the Muslim call to prayer that echoed through the town in the mornings and the evenings. And I couldn't tell you when it was that I first understood that Eliza and her children who lived across the dusty road were my friends. It is hard to know when I first noticed the diversity in Sierra Leone – its modern city buildings and its carefully crafted mud-and-thatch homes up-country. You would think I would be able to remember when it was that the river we travelled to whenever we could was a ribbon of olive light more beautiful than the Thames could ever be, and more ancient than the sound of breathing, but I can't remember because it was a gradual acclimatization. By the time I recognized what had happened, I had already been living among friends for many months, and we had picked many bunches of bananas from the tree, and the sky had lightened and darkened over the town a hundred times or more, and tragically, it was almost time to go back to where I had come from.

In Africa I learned and relearned myself. On a continent that blind Europeans had called 'dark,' I began to see how light could reveal itself in a spectrum of intense, unapologetic oranges, reds, and greens. At the risk of sounding foolish, my journey back to a land I'd never visited elevated me to a state of grace. If God exists, I found It there. It was in my shadow when the noonday sun stretched me out along the pink dust road. It was in the mouths of Sierra Leoneans when they laughed with me over *foo foo* and bitter leaf stew. It was in the hands of children scratching out their sweet responses to Macbeth in classrooms exploding with heat and necessary ambition. And it was in the dawns and dusks of a country steeped in unabashed phosphorescence. In Africa, 'dark' took on another resonance. It wasn't the dark of Conrad. Instead, 'dark' was an intensity of colour, complexions I could approximate with my own. Terrified though I had been to leave my mother's home in London, the journey to Africa taught me more than I could ever teach. I learned how to listen to the land and its people-a lesson I have tried to take with me on all my journeys, however challenging they may be.

It has been many years since I was in Africa, and the only way I have found to treasure it is by writing and painting what I saw. I plan to go back next year. This time I will take my own child with me. When he meets strangers-who-will-soon-be-friends over there, I will remind him to listen to what they say even when they are not speaking. Because, if you listen well, their quiet words are housed in the land, and the rain uncovers them, and the sun burns them to a cacophony, and the words rise up to shake our hands. And we are not strangers after all.

There is a collection of stories by Bessie Head, the South African writer, called *The Collector of Treasures*. It is a book I read frequently with my students because in it you can learn how women bless themselves by mining small treasures from the earth: another woman's smile, perhaps, or the touch of a child, or an elderly person's many stories. When I go back to Africa, I will endeavour to collect as many treasures as possible. When I unpack each invisible gift, I will place it around my house next to the photographs of my late mother and father, who still find time, however far away they may be, to speak to me. Abiding with us in our home in Virginia will be the greetings of new friends, a gorgeous African sky, and the glory-darkness of a continent alive with light.

Lucinda Roy: Go Girl! The Black Woman's Book of Adventure

(ed Elaine Lees, 1999)

My Polish Teacher's Tie

I wear a uniform, blue overall and white cap with the school logo it. Part-time catering staff that's me, £3.89 per hour. I dish out tea and buns to the teachers twice a day, and I shovel chips on to the kids' trays at dinner-time. It's not a bad job. I like the kids.

The teachers pay for their tea and buns. It's one of those schemes teachers are good at. So much into a kitty, and that entitles them to cups of tea and buns for the rest of the term. Visitors pay, too, or it wouldn't be fair. Very keen on fairness, we are, here.

It was ten-forty-five when the Head got up to speak. He sees his staff together for ten minutes once a week, and as usual he had a pile of papers in front of him. I never listen to any of it as a rule, but as I was tipping up the teapot to drain I heard him mention Poland.

I am half-Polish. They don't know that here. My name's not Polish or anything. It was my mother, she came here after the war. I spoke Polish till I was six, baby Polish full of rhymes Mum taught me. Then my father put a stop to it. 'You'll get her all mixed up, now she's going to school. What use is Polish ever going to be to her?' I can't speak it now. I've got a tape, a tape of me speaking Polish with Mum. I listen, and I think I'm going to understand what we're saying, and then I don't.

'...long-term aim is to arrange a teacher exchange – several Polish teachers are looking for pen-friends in English schools, to improve their written English... so if you're interested, the information's all here...'

He smiled, wagging the papers, and raised his eyebrows. I wrung out a cloth and wiped my surfaces. I was thinking fast. Thirteen minutes before I was due downstairs.

The meeting broke up and the Head vanished in a knot of teachers wanting to talk to him. I lifted the counter-flap, tucked my hair under the cap, and walked across. Teachers are used to getting out of the way of catering staff without really seeing them.

'Excuse me,' I said, pushing forward, 'excuse me,' and they did. Then I was in front of the Head. 'Excuse me,' I said again, and he broke off what he was saying. I saw him thinking, *trouble*. The kids chucking chips again. He stitched a nice smile on his face and said, 'Oh, er – Mrs, er – Carter. Is there a problem?'

143

'No,' I said, 'I was just wondering, could I have that address?'

'Address?'

'The Polish one, You said there was a Polish teacher who wanted an English penfriend.'

'Oh. Ah, yes. Of course.' He paused, looking at me as if it might be a trick question. 'Is it for yourself?'

'I'd like to write to a Polish teacher.'

'Oh,' he said. 'Yes. Of course, Mrs Carter.'

I took the address and smiled at him.   ❚❚

When Steve's first letter came I saw he'd taken it for granted I was a teacher. The person he had in his head when he was writing to me was an English teacher, a real professional. This person earned more money than him and had travelled and seen places and done things he'd never been able to do. He was really called Stefan, but he said he was going to call himself Steve when he wrote to me.

Jade saw the letter. 'What's that, Mum?'

'Just a letter. You can have the stamp if you want.'

In the second letter Steve told me that he wrote poetry.

'I have started a small literary magazine in our department. If you want, I am happy to send you some of our work.'

I told him about Jade. I told him about the songs my mother taught me in Polish, the ones I used to know but I'd forgotten. I didn't write anything about my job. Let him think what he wanted to think. I wasn't lying.

The first poem he sent me was about a bird in a coal mine. He sent me the English translation. This bird flew down the main shaft and got lost in the tunnels underground, then it sang and sang until it died. Everyone heard it singing, but no one could find it. I liked that poem. It made me think maybe I'd been missing something, because I hadn't read any poetry since I left school. I wrote back, *'Send me the Polish, just so I can see it.'* When the Polish came I tried it over in my head. It sounded a bit like the rhymes my mother used to sing.

At first we wrote every week, then it was twice. I used to write a bit every day then make myself wait until the middle of the week to send it. I wrote after Jade was in bed. Things would suddenly come to me. I'd write, *'Oh, Steve, I've just remembered. . .',* or *'...Do you see what I mean, Steve, or does it sound funny?'* It made it seem more like talking to him when I used his name.

He wrote me another poem. It was about being half-Polish and half-English, and the things I'd told him about speaking Polish until I was six and then forgetting it all:

'Mother, I've lost the words you gave me.
Call the police, tell them
there's a reward, I'll do anything ...'

He was going to put it in the literary magazine, *'if you have no objection, Carla'*. That was the way he wrote, always very polite. I said it was fine by me.

One day the Head stopped me and said, 'Did you ever write to that chap? The Polish teacher?'

'Yes,' I said. Nothing more. Let him think I'd written once then not bothered. Luckily, Mrs Callendar came up to talk about OFSTED.

'Ah, yes, OFSTED. Speaking of visitors,' said the Head, raising his voice the way he does so that one minute he's talking to you and the next it's a public announcement, 'I have news of progress on the Polish teachers' exchange. A teacher will be coming over from Katowice next month. His name is Stefan Jeziorny, and he will be staying with Mrs Kenward. We're most grateful to you for your hospitality, Valerie.'

Mrs Kenward flushed. The Head beamed at nobody. Stefan Jeziorny, I thought. I had clicked, even though I was so used to thinking of him as Steve. Why hadn't he said he was coming?

I dropped Jade off to tea with her friend. There was a letter waiting when I got home. I tore it open and read it with my coat still on. There was a bit about my last letter, and poetry, and then the news.

'You will know from your school, Carla, that I will come to England. I am hoping to make many contacts for the future, for other teachers who will also come to English schools. I hope, Carla, that you will introduce me to your colleagues. I will stay with an English Family who offer accommodation.'

I felt terrible. He sounded different, not like Steve. Not just polite any more, but all stiff, and a bit hurt. He must have thought I'd known about his visit from the other teachers, and I hadn't wanted to invite him to stay with me. But what was worse was that he was going to expect to meet me. Or not me, exactly, but the person he'd been writing to, who didn't really exist. *'I have been corresponding with a colleague of yours, Carla Carter,'* he'd say to the other teachers. Then he'd wait for someone to say, *'Yes, of course, Carla's here, she's expecting you.'* ▐▌

145

Colleagues don't wear blue overalls and white caps and work for £3.89 an hour. Somebody'd remember me asking the Head for his address, and there'd be a whisper running all round, followed by a horrible silence. They'd all look round at the serving-hatch and there I'd be, the big teapot in my hand and a plate of buns in front of me. And Steve'd look too. He'd still be smiling, because that's what you do in a foreign place when you don't know what's going on.

He'd think I was trying to make a fool of him, making him believe I was a teacher. Me, Carla Carter, part-time catering assistant, writing to him about poetry.   **||**

I could be off sick. I could swap with Jeannie. She could do the teachers' breaks. Or I could say Jade was ill.

No. That wouldn't work. Steve had my name, and my address. I sat down and spread out his letter again, then I went to the drawer and got all his other letters. I'd never had letters like that before and I was never going to again, not after Steve knew who I really was.

I didn't write, and Steve didn't write again either. I couldn't decide if it was because he was hurt, or because he knew he'd be seeing me soon anyway. The fuss Valerie Kenward made about having him to stay, you'd think the Pope was coming for a fortnight. I never liked her. Always holding up the queue saying she's on a diet, and then taking the biggest bun.

'If you're that bothered,' I said, 'he can come and stay in my flat, with me and Jade.' But I said it to myself, in my head. I knew he'd want to be with the other teachers.

I couldn't stop looking for letters. And then there was the poetry book I'd bought. It seemed a shame to bin it. It might come in for Jade, I thought.

A week went by, eight days, ten. Each morning I woke up and I knew something was wrong before I could remember what it was. It got worse every day until I thought, *Sod it, I'm not going to worry any more.*

The next morning-break the buns were stale. Valerie Kenward poked them, one after another. 'We ought to get our money back,' she said. But she still took one, and waited while I filled the teapot from the urn.

'How's it going?' Susie Douglas asked her.

'*Hard work!*' stage-whispered Valerie, rolling her eyes.

'He's not got much conversation, then?'

'Are you joking? All he wants to talk about is poetry. It's hell for the kids, he doesn't mean to be funny but they can't keep a straight face. It's the way he talks. Philippa had to leave the room at supper-time, and I can't say I blame her.'

You wouldn't, I thought. If ever anyone brought up their kids to be pleased with themselves, it's Valerie Kenward.

'And even when it's quite a well-known writer like Shakespeare or Shelley, you can't make out what he's on about. It's the accent.'

'He *is* Polish. I mean, how many Polish poets could you pronounce?' asked Susie.

'And his *ties!*' went on Valerie. 'You've never seen anything like them.'

I looked past both of them. I'd have noticed him before, if I hadn't been so busy. He was sitting stiffly upright, smiling in the way people smile when they don't quite understand what's going on. The Head was wagging a sheaf of papers in front of him, and talking very loudly, as if he was deaf. Steve. Stefan Jeziorny. He was wearing a brown suit with padded shoulders. It looked too big for him. His tie was wider than normal ties, and it was red with bold green squiggles on it. It was a terribly hopeful tie. His shoes had a fantastic shine on them. His face looked much too open, much too alive, as if a child Jade's age had got into an adult's body.

'Isn't that tea made *yet*?' asked Valerie.

I looked at her. 'No,' I said. 'It's not. Excuse me,' and I lifted the counter-flap and ducked past her while her mouth was still open. I walked up to where Steve was sitting. He looked round at me the way a child does when he doesn't know anyone at a party, hoping for rescue. **II**

'Hello,' I said. He jumped up, held out his hand.

'How do you do?' he asked, as if he really wanted to know. I took his hand. It was sweaty, as I'd known it would be. He was tense as a guitar string.

'I'm Carla,' I said.

'Carla?' He couldn't hide anything. I saw it all swim in his eyes. Surprise. Uncertainty. What was he going to do? And then I saw it. Pleasure. A smile lit in his eyes and ran to his mouth.

'Carla? You are Carla Carter. My penfriend.'

'Yes.'

Then he did something I still can't quite believe. He stood there holding on to my hand right in the middle of the staffroom, his big bright tie blazing, and he sang a song I knew. It went through me like a knife through butter. A Polish song. I knew it, I knew it. I knew the words and the tune. It was one of the songs my mother used to sing to

147

me. I felt my lips move. There were words in my mouth, words I didn't understand. And then I was singing, stumbling after him all the way to the end of the verse.

'Good heavens. How very remarkable. I didn't realise you were Polish, Mrs... er...' said the Head as he bumbled round us flapping his papers.

'Nor did I,' I said. But I wasn't going to waste time on the Head. I wanted to talk about poetry, I smiled at Steve. His red tie with its bold green squiggles was much too wide and much too bright. It was a flag from another country, a better country than the ones either of us lived in. 'I like your tie,' I said.

Helen Dunmore: Ice-cream (2001)

One Woman's Cup of Tea

Xinran was born in Beijing in 1958 and was a successful journalist and radio presenter in China. Since 1997 she has lived in London but she travels regularly to China where she is still well-known.

In a four-star hotel in China, one woman's cup of tea is another woman's daily wages

I was in the second-floor coffee shop of the Grand Central Hotel in Nanjing last year, waiting for the director of my old radio station. I had all my attention concentrated on my reading, when a voice spoke in my ear: 'Are you Xinran?' A cleaner was standing before me. She was polishing the dazzlingly bright metal railing beside me with a cloth, but her eyes were fixed on me.

'Yes? I'm Xinran. Is there something I can do for you?'

'No, nothing, I just wanted to tell you that the cup of tea you're drinking costs as much as my whole family earns in a day.' She turned her back on me and left.

I was stupefied. That cup of tea cost 15 yuan (£1.15) and it was the cheapest beverage in the four-star hotel. I am not wealthy: In a place like this, I could only be a tea-drinker, but she said I was drinking the daily income of her entire family. The cleaning woman and her words lingered on in my mind.

Two days later, I stopped her politely as she was leaving by the back door of the hotel. 'I saw you were at work at six o'clock this morning,' I said. 'That's really hard work.'

'It's nothing. I'm used to it. There are people who'd love to find hard labour like this and can't get it!' She told me she'd been working eight hours a day at the hotel for the best part of a year. 'Is it tiring?' I asked.

'How could it be anything else? There are a lot of cleaners in this hotel – you might not think there was that much for any one person to do, but none of us dares to stop and rest, and after eight hours we're too tired to move. But my child, my husband and the two old folk all have to eat, so I have to go to the market to buy vegetables, cook supper and do the housework.'

She said none of the cleaners took the half-hour break they were entitled to because they were scared. 'We may just get 15 yuan for a day, but we're paid by the day, and I can't do weekends either. But it was hard enough to get this job. My husband's been laid off too. If neither of us does anything, what is the family supposed to eat, and how will we get the child to school?'

They would need a huge sum of money to send her six-year-old to school the following year, she said. 'Isn't there a system of compulsory education now?' I asked.

'It says in the papers that there's compulsory education, but what school doesn't demand support fees? That's 4-5,000 yuan at the least – 10,000 for some – and no school if you don't pay. But how can a child manage without school?'

I asked her if she liked her work. 'What does it matter? I've done well to have found this job, so many can't even do that. You go to the labour exchange and look at all those people searching for a job. If an employer comes in, the people looking for work are desperate enough to tear him to pieces. There are too many out of work these days.

'I got someone to fix [this job] for me. The first three months of my wages weren't enough to cover the 'connection fees'. And I have an advantage – I'm young. The really sad ones are the women of 40 and 50 who lose their jobs: people looking for workers think they're too old. The insurance people say it's not economical to insure older people. It's awful for the women laid-off – all those people like broken bricks thrown away by the roadside. You can't make them into a wall, at most you can use them to fill in the ditches by the side of the road, but far more of them are rubbish to be carted off to the tip.'

She said her husband hadn't found another job. 'He'd rather die than do all those low jobs. You know men, always thinking about their face. Still, life is hard enough already, if you don't iron out your own frown lines, nobody else will do it for you.'

I told her I was sorry. 'Not to worry. We're different. You live for the pleasant things in life, I live because I've no choice. Goodbye.'

This one sentence really gave me food for thought. Walking in the streets of London, watching women enjoy their shopping trips, I often thought of those women in China living 'because they must'. My only comfort was that in China, many women know how to 'iron away' the 'frown lines' of life.

If we say that my cup of tea was a days wages for a woman worker, then how many days' wages are spent by the big businessmen and high-ranking officials who sit every day at the restaurant eating expensive mountain delicacies and seafood, with a new menu every day? What explanation can there be for this in a system whose slogan is to 'level out the differences between the rich and the poor'?

Xinran, 2003 (translated by Esther Tyldesley)

I Can't Forget the Girl in the Orange Dress

For three months, back in the long, hot summer of 2004, I saw her almost every day. I don't know very much about her – her age, her name, even if she is still alive. All I know is that, even now, after all this time, I can't get her out of my head.

She lived – if you could call it that – outside the sprawling British logistics base[1] of Shaibah, several kilometres south-west of Basrah City. That's where I was living and working, a member of the British Army bringing peace and stability (at least, that was the idea) to southern Iraq. Behind the wire of the camp fence, protected by roving patrols, we felt safe and sound, well-fed and comfortable, apart from the ever-present heat. It was only when we ventured out from the cosy confines of the camp that we felt in danger, travelling in no fewer than two-vehicle convoys in case of breakdown, three people per Land Rover, with at least one on 'top cover', stood up in the back and scanning the road ahead for ambushes or roadside bombs. Many had already lost their lives this way, particularly US soldiers in the north.

That is how we were travelling when I first saw the girl in the orange dress. We would take a route we called Bone – a bone-shaker of a ride, particularly for the soldiers stood up in the back. It was little more than a dirt road linking two metalled roads, and besides being a short cut was flat and exposed, giving the roadside bombers little chance to plant their deadly presents without being seen. Up on top cover, you could see for miles, out into the dusty heat haze towards the city to the east and the airport to the north.

I had been driving vehicles of one type or another for nearly 20 years by the time I went to Iraq – it made sense for me to be driving here. We would pull off the main road into Basrah and take the dogleg of Bone, Tarmac turning swiftly to rutted, compacted gravel and sand. Within a few hundred metres, she would be there, waving madly, running towards our little convoy as fast as she could from a thicket of scrubby trees no more than 30 metres from the roadside.

[1] *A logistics base deals with supplies and equipment for the Army*

151

We never, ever stopped. We would flash by at high speed, experiencing and observing her daily routine in quick flashes, like advertisements or random TV shows glimpsed while channel surfing.

The girl in the orange dress lived in a home made of plastic sheeting, a simple shelter strung between the bare trees in the thicket. She was six years old, or maybe she was 11. She was barefoot and always smiled. She had a brother, who was older or at least bigger than her, and sometimes he would be with her, running to the road, smiling and waving. More often than not she was alone. She stayed at her roadside 'house' all day and all night, or maybe came there during the day, sent by parents to beg what she could from the British soldiers. The soldiers who never, ever stopped.

We talked about the girl often. Those of us with children of our own became mildly obsessed with her existence, comparing her harsh reality with the comfort she would find in our own homes – my oldest son, waking on his seventh birthday around the same time I first saw her, surrounded by presents. I'm sure she would have appreciated even one of the toys he didn't play with any more, a teddy bear or a car. Even more, his birthday meal.

So I hatched a plan. I had no toys to give her, but I could put together a bag of food and water. Food perished very quickly outside our canteen facilities; all I could get for her were the ration packs we kept in our rucksacks in case of emergency. Would she know what to do with dehydrated food and brew kit? I didn't know – but it was worth a try.

My plan was to get one of the lads on top cover to drop the sealed bag from the back of the vehicle as we flashed by. But my plan was foiled by two things. First a young Iraqi boy was injured by a British vehicle in Basrah City, which resulted in an official ban on giving food and water to civilians. Then I was transferred from Shaibah to a new job at Basrah airport – I would no longer make the daily run along Bone.

My last journey from Shaibah to the airport was made by helicopter due to a leg injury sustained on an operation the week before. Sweeping over Bone from the air, I saw a flash of orange, and then she was gone.

Noel K Hannan, Guardian (2006)

Seeing Things
Activities

Note to Sixth-Grade Self
Before Reading

What Kind of Writing?

- Look at the statements below. What kind of text do you think they might come from? Why?

    - Do not run in the corridors.

    - Have the right equipment with you.

    - Walk on the left when going upstairs.

    - Stay silent during fire drill.

- Now look at these extracts from the text you are going to read. In what ways do the extracts seem similar or different to the statements above?

    - On Wednesdays wear a skirt.

    - At three-thirty stand outside with the others and take the number seven bus uptown.

    - Pay attention.

    - When it is time for the boys to pick, do not bite your hangnails.

    - Do not leave your bag on the bus.

    - Let all the misery fall out of your chest.

- Discuss with a partner what kind of text you think the extracts are from.

- Share your ideas as a class.

──────── During Reading ────────

Places to 'pause' during reading are marked with a pause button symbol like this:

II

'Do not look at the boys.'

■ Read up to 'Do not look at the boys.' **II** Although this text is a short story, the writer has used some of the features of instruction writing or rule writing. Look back over what you have read so far with a partner and see which features of instruction or rule writing you can see. You might notice:

– Imperatives: these are verbs that give orders such as 'Be (quiet)' or 'Walk (slowly)'.

– Sentences beginning 'Don't...'

– Short, to the point sentences such as 'On Wednesdays wear a skirt'.

'When she asks you how your afternoon went, lie.'

■ Read up to 'When she asks you how your afternoon went, lie.' **II**

■ Now think about why the writer might have used features of instruction or rule writing. Discuss this first with your partner and then as a whole class. You could use the ideas below to get your discussion started.

– The writer wants to show that, as well as the written rules in school, there are also lots of unwritten rules[1] you have to keep to survive.

– The writer hopes her story will help other teenagers avoid the mistakes she made and fit in better with people of the same age.

– The writer is using the story to explore what it would be like to give herself instructions for how to behave at difficult times.

– The writer has chosen an unusual style for a short story to make it more interesting to read.

– The writer wants to show that, even when you try to follow the unwritten rules[1] of being a teenager, you can still get bullied if certain students decide they don't like you.

[1]*Unwritten rules are the ones everybody in a particular group seems to know about even though they haven't been written down. They are not created by people in authority (like teachers, or the government). For example, in school there are often unwritten rules about what to wear or what music to listen to if you want to belong to a particular group. Certain kinds of behaviour, such as 'grassing' on someone, or being a teacher's pet, might be against the unwritten rules.*

'You blind, proud, stupid, poor dunce.'

■ Read up to 'You blind, proud, stupid, poor dunce.' **II**

What Happens Next?

In the next part of the story, the narrator decides to take the dress to school so that everyone can see it is real. Cara and Patricia see her with the bag that has the dress in it.

1. Role play

■ In a group of three, you are going to role play what you think might happen. Before you start, think about what you already know about the characters of the narrator, Patricia and Cara. How might each one react?

■ Show some of your role plays to the class and discuss any similarities and differences in the ways you chose to play the scene.

2. Continuing the story

■ Now write 1-3 paragraphs telling your own version of the next part of the story. You could use ideas from your own role play, or one of the other role plays you watched to help you if you wish. Try to use some of the features of instruction or rule writing so that your part of the story would fit with the way the rest of the story is written.

■ Your teacher will read out some of your versions, along with two or three paragraphs of the next section of the story. Discuss whether anyone has used the style so well that it is difficult to tell the difference between their version and the original.

'... the houses all around them in splinters'

■ Read up to 'the houses all around them in splinters, people and animals dead.' **II**

■ How does your version of the story compare with what the writer decided to do?

Predicting the Ending

■ In the next part of the story, Eric Cassio calls round to the narrator's house. As a class, discuss what sort of ending the story might have. Do you think it will end happily, sadly or some mixture of the two?

■ Read to the end of the story and discuss how your predictions compare with the ending the writer chose.

Seeing Things in the Dark

——————— Before Reading ———————

About Sierra Leone

The setting for this text is Sierra Leone. Before you read, it might be helpful to know a little about the country.

Sierra Leone is a country in West Africa. The country suffered ten years of civil war, which finally came to an end in 2002. Although the country is slowly trying to rebuild itself after so many years of fighting, the problems of poverty, tribal rivalry and corruption that caused the war are not easy to solve.

The country is rich in diamonds, but the diamonds tend to make only a few people in the country rich. The government is trying to crack down on the smuggling of the gems, known as 'blood diamonds' because of their role in causing war.

The main languages are English and Krio, with most people also speaking one or more tribal languages as well. Krio is a Creole language. This means it is a mixture of English and local languages which has become a language in its own right. The main religions are Islam, local tribal beliefs and Christianity.

——————— During Reading ———————

Track the Changes

In this text a woman changes as a result of her experiences in Sierra Leone. She has gone to the country as a volunteer teacher in a school for girls.

■ Track the way Lucinda Roy changes using a chart like the one on page 157. As you read, fill in the final column of the chart to show what the writer is thinking or feeling at each point.

Quotation from the text	What do you think she is thinking or feeling at this point?
After all my dreams of making a difference, I had arrived in West Africa with too much baggage to be any good to anyone.	
I lived in West Africa, but I wasn't really there.	
I had tunnel vision. At the end of the tunnel was a letter from home.	
Nothing. No letters from home.	
In Krio, he demanded money, forced me to look again at his pitiful limb.	
I never found him, but there were others who took his place.	
Little by little, the British fog began to rise.	
By the time I had recognised what had happened...it was almost time to go back where I came from.	

—————— After Reading ——————

'My Holiday Changed My Life'

■ Look back over your chart and, as a class, discuss how you think the writer changed while she was in Sierra Leone.

■ Imagine you are going to interview Lucinda Roy about her experiences for a television travel show called 'My Holiday Changed My Life'. Read the memo below from the producer who has asked you to do the interview, and bear her instructions in mind as you write your interview questions.

Memo from the producer of 'My Holiday Changed My Life'

Thank you for agreeing to interview Lucinda Roy about her travel experience in Sierra Leone. As you know, this is for a new slot in the programme in which we talk to people who have been travelling, not on holiday, but to do volunteer work and to try to make a difference to the lives of local people.

We call ourselves 'the travel show with a more adventurous spirit'. Our viewers are not interested in lying on beaches or by hotel swimming pools. Our most recent audience research shows that our viewers prefer environmentally responsible holidays and are interested in travelling for months rather than weeks. Many have done volunteer work abroad or are thinking about doing so in the future. In our recent audience survey, most decided that the statements 'For an adventure', 'For a life changing experience' and 'To learn about other cultures and local people' best fitted their reasons for travelling. A sizeable minority of our viewers watch the show because they like to fantasize about a life-changing travel experience, even though they do not have the time, the money or the guts to take such a journey at the moment.

When you interview Lucinda Roy we would like you to think carefully about what would interest our audience. The slot lasts for one minute and we would suggest, as a rough guideline, that you prepare around seven to ten questions. Make sure that your questions cannot be answered with a simple 'yes' or 'no'. A minute of someone answering 'yes' or 'no' is not thrilling television!

Best wishes,

Aysha Wilson

■ As a class, decide on the main points from the memo that you will need to bear in mind when writing your questions.

■ Draw up your list of questions, thinking about what the viewers of 'My Holiday Changed My Life' might want to know. Make sure that all your questions can be answered by reading the text.

■ With a partner, take it in turns to role play the interviewer asking your questions and the interviewee, Lucinda Roy, answering them.

■ As a class, watch some of the best interviews and discuss how well you think they would appeal to the target audience of 'My Holiday Changed My Life'.

My Polish Teacher's Tie

Before Reading

The Title

■ Write the title of the text on a piece of paper. With a partner, brainstorm any questions the title raises for you and make some predictions about the story.

During Reading

'I took the address and smiled at him'

■ Read as far as 'I took the address and smiled at him.' **II** With a partner, discuss why you think Carla (Mrs Carter) wants to write to a Polish teacher.

'Yes, of course, Carla's here, she's expecting you'.

Stefan/Steve does not say in his letter that he is offended by the fact that she has not invited him to stay but Carla reads between the lines and thinks he sounds 'Not just polite anymore but all stiff, and a bit hurt.'

■ With a partner, look back at the extract from the letter. Underline any words or phrases that seem to show that Stefan/Steve was 'hurt'. As a class discuss whether you agree with Carla that he sounds hurt.

■ As a class, discuss how Carla might feel about the possibility of finally meeting Stefan/Steve.

'Carla Carter, part-time catering assistant'

■ Read as far as 'Carla Carter, part-time catering assistant, writing to him about poetry.' **II**

■ Imagine you are Carla's friend. She tells you why she is embarrassed to meet Stefan/Steve and asks your advice on how to handle the situation.

■ With a partner, role play the conversation between Carla and her friend.

'He looked round at me the way a child does'

■ Read as far as 'He looked round at me the way a child does'. **II**

■ Write the next paragraph as Carla and Stefan/Steve meet.

■ Listen to some of the paragraphs being read aloud. Discuss which seem to fit best with the story so far, and why.

'… a better country'

■ Read to the end of the story. Carla describes the Polish teacher's tie as 'a flag from another country, a better country than the ones either of us lived in.' First with a partner and then as a class, discuss what you think she means by this.

■ Thinking about the title and the ending of the story, discuss as a class what you think the Polish teacher's tie represents in the story. You could use some of the prompts below to get your discussion started if you wish.

- The tie represents the misunderstandings that can happen between two cultures.

- The tie is a way to show how snobby and unfriendly the teachers are towards the Polish teacher.

- Because the tie is bright and cheerful, it represents the way things could be if people from different countries took the time to get to know each other the way Carla and Stefan/Steve do.

- The tie represents the way people judge by appearances and how limiting and unfair this is.

———————— After Reading ————————

Carla's Embarrassment

1. Why is she embarrassed about meeting Stefan/Steve?

■ Decide which of the statements below is the most likely explanation for why Carla is embarrassed about meeting Stefan/Steve, or come up with a reason of your own.

Carla is embarrassed because:

- she lied to Stefan/Steve in her letters

- she thinks the teachers will make fun of her because she is not a teacher

- she does not think she is as good as a teacher, so Stefan/Steve will be disappointed in her.

■ Find examples or quotations in the text to back up the statement you have chosen. Share your thoughts as a class.

2. Carla's realisation

■ As a class, discuss whether you think Carla had any reason to be embarrassed and what she has realised by the end of the story.

Your Own Writing

Exchanging Letters

Imagine that when he returns to Poland, Stefan/Steve and Carla exchange letters about their meeting. Choose one of the activities below.

■ Write a letter from the Polish teacher and a reply from Carla in which they describe the meeting from their different perspectives.

■ Divide the class into two halves, with half writing a letter from Carla to Stefan/Steve and the other half writing a letter from Stefan/Steve to Carla, each giving their account of the meeting. Read out some of the letters and discuss the different points of view the two characters might have on the same incident.

'Mother, I've lost the words you gave me.'

Stefan/Steve writes Carla a poem about the fact that she spoke Polish until the age of six but has now almost forgotten the language. The first line is 'Mother, I've lost the words you gave me.'

■ Write the rest of the poem for Carla, or use the first line to start you off on a poem or short story using your own ideas.

One Woman's Cup of Tea

——— Before Reading ———

What Could You Do With £1.15?

■ As a class, brainstorm as many things as you can that you could do with £1.15.

A Cup of Tea

■ The headline for the article is 'One Woman's Cup of Tea'. As a class, brainstorm any well-known phrases or sayings the title might remind you of.

——— After Reading ———

The Headline

Xinran's headline 'One Woman's Cup of Tea' might remind the reader of several different well-known phrases.

■ Have a look at the phrases below and add in any you came up with before reading.

■ As a class, discuss what each phrase means and when it might be used.

– One man's meat is another man's poison.

– For the price of a cup of tea...

– It's not my cup of tea.

– I wouldn't do it for all the tea in China.

■ On your own, choose two of the phrases and think about why Xinran might have wanted to bring them to mind for the reader. Make some notes and be prepared to feed back to the class. Some ideas for the first phrase have been given to you below.

One man's meat is another man's poison.

This makes me think about the fact that the two women in the article have such different lives. The phrase is usually used to show how people choose different things because they have different tastes, but in this article the poor woman has no choice. She just has to try to manage on her small wage.

What Kind of Writing?

- As a class, revise some of the key features of writing that informs, writing that argues and writing that persuades. Descriptions of different kinds of writing can be found at the back of the book (pages 236-239) if you need them.

- Work in threes. Discuss whether you think this is a piece of writing that informs, argues or persuades. Find evidence from the text to support your view including examples of the following:

  - features which are typical of this kind of writing

  - features which are not typical of this type of writing.

- Explain what kind of writing you think the article is and feed back your evidence to the class.

- As a class, discuss how far you agree or disagree about what kind of writing this is, or whether you think the piece is doing more than one job.

—— Your Own Writing ——

Inequalities

- Think about an area of life in which there is an inequality that bothers you, for instance, the lack of a girls' football team in your local area or the fact that children don't seem to have the same rights as adults.

- Research some facts about this situation.

- Think of, or invent, a personal anecdote that would show this inequality.

- Write an article about the situation, starting your piece of writing with the anecdote. You could use features of writing to inform, argue or persuade to get people to realize the unfairness of the situation. Your article should be aimed at people your age and could be written for the school magazine or another magazine for young people.

Extension Work

Cultural Context

■ In groups of three, look at the following extracts with explanations. In your group, discuss which of the extracts you were able to understand just by reading the text or because of what you already know about China, and which of the explanations helped you to understand the article better.

1. 'It says in the papers that there's compulsory education, but what school doesn't demand support fees.'

China's media is controlled by the government. Journalists generally report the government's version of what is happening, which is often propaganda rather then the truth.

2. 'You know men, always thinking about their face.'

'Face' could be translated as 'pride', 'honour', 'respect' or 'good reputation'. In Chinese society it is considered very important to avoid losing face or causing someone else to lose face. There are lots of ways to increase 'face', for example avoiding making a mistake, acting in an honourable way or receiving a compliment.

3. 'What explanation can there be for this in a system whose slogan is to 'level out the differences between the rich and the poor'?'

China is a Communist country. The Communist ideal is to create an economic or political system based on the sharing of all work and property by the whole community so that everyone is equal. In practice it is very difficult to create a truly Communist system, and China has not managed to do it.

I Can't Forget the Girl in the Orange Dress

──── Before Reading ────

Predictions

■ Work in a group of three. Each person should take responsibility for one of the groups of six words below. Look at your group of words. What you notice about them?

Word group one					
emergency	injury	harsh	beg	danger	barefoot

Word group two					
ambushes	bombs	peace	patrols	civilian	camp

Word group three					
comfort	presents	safe	well-fed	comfortable	smiling

■ Form new groups of three with other people looking at the same group of words as you. Look at the group of words you have been allocated. They are all taken from the text you are about to read. Discuss what you notice about the group of words. Make as many predictions as you can about the text.

■ Return to your original group of three and share some of the ideas and predictions from your discussions.

■ As a class, make new predictions, based on your discussions about all the groups of words.

──── During Reading ────

Your Word Group

■ As you read the text, look out for the six words you had in your word group and how they are used in the article, for example whose situation is being described?

After Reading

Your Response

1. On your own

◼ Think to yourself for a moment about your response to the text. What did it make you think or feel? Share your thoughts with the person sitting next to you.

2. As a class

◼ As a class, discuss any ways in which the text fitted your predictions and any surprises.

3. In a small group

◼ Working in your group of three, discuss which of the following statements you most agree with and explain why.

The soldier who is telling the story sympathises with the girl because they both have to deal with the harsh reality of the war.	1

The soldier who is telling the story feels guilty about being protected in the camp.	2

The soldier thinks his own son is spoilt.	3

The soldier thinks his son does not realise how lucky he is.	4

The soldier wishes he could have helped the girl to have the kind of life his son has.	5

The soldier wishes he could do more to help the people of Iraq but can't, so he focuses on trying to help this one girl.	6

The soldier wants the reader to understand what a hard time he had in Iraq.	7

The soldier wants the reader to understand how hard life is for ordinary Iraqis.	8

Your Own Writing

Writing About Your Response

■ Write between two and five paragraphs about your personal response to the text. To help you to get started you could use one of the statements above or one or two of the sentence starters below.

- – This text made me think about...

- – What I really liked about this article was the way that...

- – I thought... because...

- – When I read the sentence '...' it made me feel...

- – When I finished reading the article I wanted to...

- – I think Noel K Hannan wanted people who read his article to think/feel...

Working With More Than One Text

Comparing 'I Can't Forget the Girl in the Orange Dress' with 'One Woman's Cup of Tea'

■ Draw a chart like the one below and fill in as many similarities and differences as you can. Some ideas have been suggested to get you started.

	I Can't Forget	One Woman's Cup of Tea
What the piece is about		
The purpose of the piece	Makes a point about inequalities in life. Gives a personal side to the war in Iraq. Shows a caring side to the soldiers fighting there.	
The opening	The writer refers to the girl as 'her'. This is because he never knew her name but it also makes her seem mysterious.	
The writer's thoughts and feelings		
Using an anecdote	The writer uses the story of the girl in the orange dress to make us think about all the children in her situation and how lucky most children in Britain are in comparison.	
The use of the first person		Xinran uses the first person ('I') because she makes her point using a personal story. This draws the reader in because we tend to be more interested in personal stories than in arguments about only facts and statistics.
The ending		

Your Own Writing

Writing a Comparison

You are going to use your chart to help you write two paragraphs comparing the two pieces of writing. Use the instructions to help you.

1. Make a point

■ First choose a point from your chart about the openings. Now write a paragraph about the opening of 'I Can't Forget the Girl in the Orange Dress', using the chart to help you. In your paragraph you should: make a point; support what you say with some evidence (a quotation or example) from the text; explain the effect on the reader. For example, you could write:

Noel K Hannan refers to the girl in the orange dress simply as 'her'. This is because he never discovers her name but it also makes her seem mysterious. The reader wants to read on to find out who this girl is and why she has made such a strong impression on the writer.

2. Make a comparison

■ Now write a second paragraph on the same point but this time on 'One Woman's Cup of Tea', using your chart to help you. Decide whether the point you are making is a similarity or a difference. If it is a similarity, use a connective such as 'similarly', 'in the same way', or 'also' in your paragraph. If your point is a difference, use a connective word or phrase such as 'on the other hand', 'whereas' or 'however'. For example:

The opening of 'One Woman's Cup of Tea' also uses a mystery person to raise questions in the reader's mind so that they want to read on. The reader does not know who the cleaner is or why she speaks to Xinran.

Or

Whereas the girl in the orange dress is only seen from a distance, the cleaner in 'One Woman's Cup of Tea' speaks to Xinran. As a result, the things Xinran tells us about her life, such as how much she earns, are facts rather than the writer having to fill in the gaps from their imagination.

3. Writing a comparative essay

■ Write about some of the other points on your chart. Add an introduction and conclusion to make an essay comparing the two pieces. Don't feel limited by the points on the chart, you could add ideas and points of your own.

The Editorial Meeting

For this work you will need to have read at least three of the pieces in this section. You are going to work in small groups. The groups should have the same number of people as the number of texts you have read in this section, as each person is going to represent one of the texts. Follow the instructions below for preparing for and running an editorial meeting to make your decision.

■ In small groups, imagine you have been given the job of editing this section of the anthology. You have been asked to cut out one of the pieces.

1. Preparation: 40 minutes

This section of the anthology is called 'Seeing Things'.

■ In your small group, discuss the questions that follow.

  – What does the title remind you of, or make you think of?

  – Why might this title have been chosen for this section?

  – How does the title fit the texts you have read in this section?

■ Now each person in your group should re-read one of the texts. As you read, make notes to suggest why you think this piece of writing should *stay* in this section of the anthology. Think about some of the questions below.

  – What makes this an effective or powerful piece of writing?

  – What did you enjoy about this piece?

  – How does the text fit in with your ideas about the title of the section? For example, how does it show someone 'seeing things'?

2. The meeting: 15 minutes

You have 15 minutes to decide which piece to cut.

■ Each of you should explain why you think your piece should stay in the anthology. You should then have a discussion and decide which piece to cut.

■ Compare your decisions with others in the class.

Touching the Void

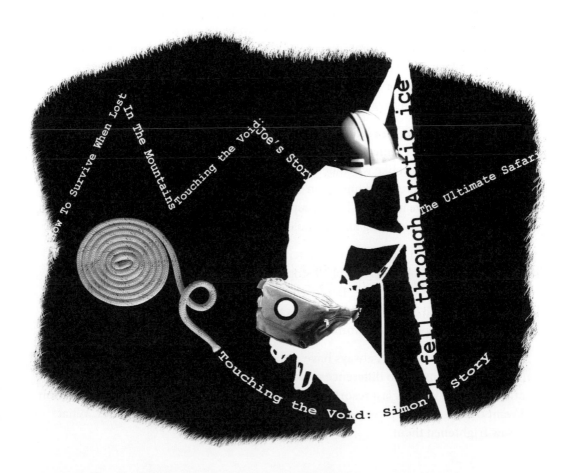

How To Survive When Lost In The Mountains

Touching the Void: Joe's Story

fell through Arctic ice

The Ultimate Safari

Touching the Void: Simon's Story

I Fell Through Arctic Ice

I have travelled 11,000 Arctic miles with dogs, summer and winter. They've been my life. There are fewer than 300 purebred Canadian Eskimo dogs left in the world and I had 15 of them. I sank all my love and money into those dogs, proud to keep the breed's working talents alive. I learnt from the best, guys who in the 1980s had crossed Antarctica and made it to the North Pole with dogs, perfectionists who knew all there was to know. I watched, listened, kept my mouth shut, and one day decided to go it alone. It felt a natural progression.

Alone, it's always dangerous. Something was bound to go wrong one day, and on Sunday March 5 last year it did. Moving over Amundsen Gulf in the Northwest Passage, sea ice gave way. Everything was sinking: my dogs, my sled and me. We kicked for our lives. Powerful Arctic Ocean currents dragged vast sheets of sea ice. Underwater, I couldn't find the hole I had fallen through and had to make one, punching, then breathing again as ice and sea water clashed against my face.

Polar bears eat people, and swim to kill. We'd crossed bear tracks an hour before going through the ice. I remember thinking, did the bastard follow us? Was he under us now? What will it feel like when he bites? The floe edge was a mile away, this a busy hunting area where bears bludgeon seals twice my size. Frantic, I ripped off my mittens. Trying to save my dogs, I was prepared to lose my hands to savage cold. It wasn't enough. Soon drowning and the cold had killed all but one of them.

Out of the water I stripped off sodden, icing-up clothing. The cold was brutal. My limbs and head shook uncontrollably. I stopped shivering, indicating I was severely hypothermic. I was slowly dying. Barely conscious, I pulled on my down suit with fingers that knocked like wood. My blood was freezing. Human consciousness is lost when the body temperature plummets below 30°C. I was heading for oblivion.

My satellite phone failed. I always have a phone backed up with a ground to air VHF transceiver, but it made no difference – I knew no plane was flying over. I flipped my location beacon. This is a last resort. To flip it means I'm in a life-threatening situation and want out. In the end three polar bear hunters came out on snowmobiles. What they saw frightened them.

I had fourth-degree frostbite, the worst form. My fingers were covered in deathly black blisters, my hands freezing to the bone. The pain when it thaws is colossal, at the top of the human tolerance scale, like a huge invisible parasite with a million fangs. The agony was suffocating; I writhed with it, wild for relief.

Heavy doses of morphine helped to dull the pain for two months. The side-effects included dreams, hallucinations, flashbacks – and constipation.

My fingers were debrided, scalpels cutting dead meat off thumbs and fingers. It hurt. Fingernails dropped off and smelt funny, and tendons stiffened. Physiotherapy was agony, but I wanted my hands back so badly and to endure meant to get better. My fingers looked a bloody mess, distorted and gnarled. They were always disturbingly cold. I was told the longer we waited, the better: even dead-looking fingers can recover.

Exercising my hands took up all my days – and within minutes they would stiffen up, giving the impression they were dying on me. I kept going, though, and one day I clasped a cup with my right hand. I was so excited. The first time I went out in the sun, my fingers turned blue. Without fingerprint ridges, picking up coins was difficult. Coins felt freezing, copper ones less so.

Soon the time to thaw before the saw was up. The surgeon cut a tip as if sharpening a pencil. I felt nothing. It jolted me to learn that the fingertip was dead. It was the only part still black, solid and stone-cold; if it wasn't removed, I'd have been susceptible to dry gangrene. It had to go.

I left hospital with 27 stitches and a metal plate on one stub-ended finger. Surgeons described my recovery as 'inexplicable' – I had been expected to lose both hands.

So what now? My dogs and I were inseparable; I miss them desperately. All I want is dog hairs on my clothes again. The plan is a move to Greenland. It's time to live again.

Gary Rolfe, Guardian (2007)

173

How To Survive When Lost in the Mountains

The number one cause of death when lost in the mountains is hypothermia – humans are basically tropical animals. Staying calm in the face of darkness, loneliness, and the unknown will greatly increase your chances of survival. Eighty percent of mountain survival is your reaction to fear, 10 percent is your survival gear, and the other 10 percent is knowing how to use it. Always tell someone else where you are going and when you will return.

1. Do not panic.

If you told someone where you were going, search and rescue teams will be looking for you. (In general, teams will search only during daylight hours for adults, but will search around the clock for children who are alone.)

2. Find shelter, and stay warm and dry.

Exerting yourself unnecessarily – like dragging heavy logs to build a shelter – will make you sweat and make you cold. Use the shelter around you before trying to construct one. If you are in a snow-covered area, you may be able to dig a cave in deep snow for shelter and protection from the wind. A snow trench may be a better idea – it requires less exertion. Simply use something to dig a trench, get in it, and cover it with branches or leaves. You should attempt to make your shelter in the middle of the mountain if possible. Stay out of the valleys – cold air falls, and the valley floor can be the coldest spot on the mountain.

3. Signal rescuers for help.

The best time to signal rescuers is during the day, with a signaling device or three fires in a triangle. Signal for help from the highest point possible – it will be easier for rescuers to see you, and any sound you make will travel farther. Build three smoky fires and put your blanket – gold side facing out, if it is a space blanket – on the ground.

In snow-covered country, build a snow cave or a snow trench for shelter and warmth. Use dead leaves and branches for insulation.

4. Do not wander far.

It will make finding you more difficult, as search teams will be trying to retrace your path and may miss you if you have gone off in a different direction. Searchers often wind up finding a vehicle with no one in it because the driver has wandered off.

5. If you get frostbite, do not rewarm the affected area until you're out of danger.

You can walk on frostbitten feet, but once you warm the area and can feel the pain, you will not want to walk anywhere. Try to protect the frostbitten area and keep it dry until you are rescued.

HOW TO PREPARE

You must dress properly before entering a wilderness area. Layer your clothing in the following manner:

FIRST (INNER) LAYER: long underwear, preferably polypropylene. This provides only slight insulation – its purpose is to draw moisture off your skin.

SECOND (MIDDLE) LAYER: something to trap and create warm 'dead air' space, such as a down parka.

THIRD (OUTER) LAYER: a Gore-Tex or other brand of breathable jacket that allows moisture out but not in. Dry insulation is key to your survival. Once you are wet, it is very difficult to get dry.

Make sure you have the following items in your survival kit, and that you know how to use them (reading the instructions for the first time in the dark wilderness is not recommended):

A HEAT SOURCE. Bring several boxes of waterproof matches, as well as a lighter. Trioxane – a small, light, chemical heat source that the Army uses – is recommended. Trioxane packs can be picked up in outdoor and military surplus stores. Dryer lint is also highly flammable and very lightweight.

SHELTER. Carry a small space blanket, which has a foil-like coating that insulates you. Get one that is silver on one side (for warmth) and orange-gold on the other, which can be used for signaling. The silver side is not a good color to signal with. It can be mistaken for ice or mineral rock. The orange-gold color does not occur in nature and will not be mistaken for anything else.

A SIGNALING DEVICE. A small mirror works well, as do flares or a whistle, which carries much farther than a voice.

FOOD. Pack carbohydrates: bagels, trail mix, granola bars, and so on. Proteins need heat to break down and require more water for digestion.

Joshua Piven: Worst-Case Scenario Survival Handbook (2000)

The Ultimate Safari

The African Adventure Lives On...You can do it!
The ultimate safari or expedition
With leaders who know Africa.
Travel Advertisement, The Observer, London, 27/11/88

That night our mother went to the shop and she didn't come back. Ever. What happened? I don't know. My father also had gone away one day and never come back; but he was fighting in the war. We were in the war, too, but we were children, we were like our grandmother and grandfather, we didn't have guns. The people my father was fighting – the bandits, they are called by our government – ran all over the place and we ran away from them like chickens chased by dogs. We didn't know where to go. Our mother went to the shop because someone said you could get some oil for cooking. We were happy because we hadn't tasted oil for a long time; perhaps she got the oil and someone knocked her down in the dark and took that oil from her. Perhaps she met the bandits. If you meet them, they will kill you. Twice they came to our village and we ran and hid in the bush and when they'd gone we came back and found they had taken everything; but the third time they came back there was nothing to take, no oil, no food, so they burned the thatch and the roofs of our houses fell in. My mother found some pieces of tin and we put those up over part of the house. We were waiting there for her that night she never came back.

We were frightened to go out, even to do our business, because the bandits did come. Not into our house – without a roof it must have looked as if there was no one in it, everything gone – but all through the village. We heard people screaming and running. We were afraid even to run, without our mother to tell us where. I am the middle one, the girl, and my little brother clung against my stomach with his arms round my neck and his legs round my waist like a baby monkey to its mother. All night my first-born brother kept in his hand a broken piece of wood from one of our burnt house-poles. It was to save himself if the bandits found him.

We stayed there all day. Waiting for her. I don't know what day it was; there was no school, no church any more in our village, so you didn't know whether it was a Sunday or a Monday.

177

When the sun was going down, our grandmother and grandfather came. Someone from our village had told them we children were alone, our mother had not come back. I say 'grandmother' before 'grandfather' because it's like that: our grandmother is big and strong, not yet old, and our grandfather is small, you don't know where he is, in his loose trousers, he smiles but he hasn't heard what you're saying, and his hair looks as if he's left it full of soap suds. Our grandmother took us – me, the baby, my first-born brother, our grandfather – back to her house and we were all afraid (except the baby, asleep on our grandmother's back) of meeting the bandits on the way. We waited a long time at our grandmother's place. Perhaps it was a month. We were hungry. Our mother never came. While we were waiting for her to fetch us our grandmother had no food for us, no food for our grandfather and herself. A woman with milk in her breasts gave us some for my little brother, although at our house he used to eat porridge, same as we did. Our grandmother took us to look for wild spinach but everyone else in her village did the same and there wasn't a leaf left.

Our grandfather, walking a little behind some young men, went to look for our mother but didn't find her. Our grandmother cried with other women and I sang the hymns with them. They brought a little food – some beans – but after two days there was nothing again. Our grandfather used to have three sheep and a cow and a vegetable garden but the bandits had long ago taken the sheep and the cow, because they were hungry, too; and when planting time came our grandfather had no seed to plant.

So they decided – our grandmother did; our grandfather made little noises and rocked from side to side, but she took no notice – we would go away. We children were pleased. We wanted to go away from where our mother wasn't and where we were hungry. We wanted to go where there were no bandits and there was food. We were glad to think there must be such a place; away.

Our grandmother gave her church clothes to someone in exchange for some dried mealies[1] and she boiled them and tied them in a rag. We took them with us when we went and she thought we would get water from the rivers but we didn't come to any river and we got so thirsty we had to turn back. Not all the way to our grandparents' place but to a village where there was a pump. She opened the basket where she carried some clothes and the mealies and she sold her shoes to buy a big plastic container for water. I said, *Gogo*, how will you go to church now even without shoes, but she said we had a long journey and too much to carry. At that village we met other people who were also going away. We joined them because they seemed to know where that was better than we did.

To get there we had to go through the Kruger Park[2]. We knew about the Kruger Park. A kind of whole country of animals – elephants, lions, jackals, hyenas, hippos,

[1] *Mealies = maize/sweetcorn*
[2] *An enormous reserve for wild animals in South Africa*

crocodiles, all kinds of animals. We had some of them in our own country, before the war (our grandfather remembers; we children weren't born yet) but the bandits kill the elephants and sell their tusks, and the bandits and our soldiers have eaten all the buck. There was a man in our village without legs – a crocodile took them off, in our river; but all the same our country is a country of people, not animals. We knew about the Kruger Park because some of our men used to leave home to work there in the places where white people come to stay and look at the animals.

So we started to go away again. There were women and other children like me who had to carry the small ones on their backs when the women got tired. A man led us into the Kruger Park; are we there yet, are we there yet, I kept asking our grandmother. Not yet, the man said, when she asked him for me. He told us we had to take a long way to get round the fence, which he explained would kill you, roast off your skin the moment you touched it, like the wires high up on poles that give electric light in our towns. I've seen that sign of a head without eyes or skin or hair on an iron box at the mission hospital we used to have before it was blown up.

When I asked the next time, they said we'd been walking in the Kruger Park for an hour. But it looked just like the bush we'd been walking through all day, and we hadn't seen any animals except the monkeys and birds which live around us at home, and a tortoise that, of course, couldn't get away from us. My first-born brother and the other boys brought it to the man so it could be killed and we could cook and eat it. He let it go because he told us we could not make a fire; all the time we were in the Park we must not make a fire because the smoke would show we were there. Police, wardens, would come and send us back where we came from. He said we must move like animals among the animals, away from the roads, away from the white people's camps. And at that moment I heard – I'm sure I was the first to hear – cracking branches and the sound of something parting grasses and I almost squealed because I thought it was the police, wardens – the people he was telling us to look out for – who had found us already. And it was an elephant, and another elephant, and more elephants, big blots of dark moved wherever you looked between the trees. They were curling their trunks round the red leaves of the Mopane trees and stuffing them into their mouths. The babies leant against their mothers. The almost grown-up ones wrestled like my first-born brother with his friends – only they used trunks instead of arms. I was so interested I forgot to be afraid. The man said we should just stand still and be quiet while the elephants passed. They passed very slowly because elephants are too big to need to run from anyone.

The buck ran from us. They jumped so high they seemed to fly. The warthogs stopped dead, when they heard us, and swerved off the way a boy in our village used to zigzag on the bicycle his father had brought back from the mines. We followed the animals to where they drank. When they had gone, we went to their water-holes.

179

We were never thirsty without finding water, but the animals ate, ate all the time. Whenever you saw them they were eating, grass, trees, roots. And there was nothing for us. The mealies were finished. The only food we could eat was what the baboons ate, dry little figs full of ants that grow along the branches of the trees at the rivers. It was hard to be like the animals. **‖**

When it was very hot during the ay we would find lions lying asleep. They were the colour of the grass and we didn't see them at first but the man did, and he led us back and a long way round where they slept. I wanted to lie down like the lions. My little brother was getting thin but he was very heavy. When our grandmother looked for me, to put him on my back, I tried not to see. My first-born brother stopped talking; and when we rested he had to be shaken to get up again, as if he was just like our grandfather, he couldn't hear. I saw flies crawling on our grandmother's face and she didn't brush them off; I was frightened. I picked a palm leaf and chased them.

We walked at night as well as by day. We could see the fires where the white people were cooking in the camps and we could smell the smoke and the meat. We watched the hyenas with their backs that slope as if they're ashamed, slipping through the bush after the smell. If one turned its head, you saw it had big brown shining eyes like our own, when we looked at each other in the dark. The wind brought voices in our own language from the compounds where the people who work in the camps live. A woman among us wanted to go to them at night and ask them to help us. They can give us the food from the dustbins, she said, she started wailing and our grandmother had to grab her and put a hand over her mouth. The man who led us had told us that we must keep out of the way of our people who worked at the Kruger Park; if they helped us they would lose their work. If they saw us, all they could do was pretend we were not there; they had seen only animals. **‖**

Sometimes we stopped to sleep for a little while at night. We slept close together. I don't know which night it was – because we were walking, walking, any time, all the time – we heard the lions very near. Not groaning loudly the way they did far off. Panting, like we do when we run, but it's a different kind of panting: you can hear they're not running, they're waiting, somewhere near. We all rolled closer together, on top of each other, the ones on the edge fighting to get into the middle. I was squashed against a woman who smelled bad because she was afraid but I was glad to hold tight on to her. I prayed to God to make the lions take someone on the edge and go. I shut my eyes not to see the tree from which a lion might jump right into the middle of us, where I was. The man who led us jumped up instead, and beat on the tree with a dead branch. He had taught us never to make a sound but he shouted. He shouted at the lions like a drunk man shouting at nobody, in our village. The lions went away. We heard them groaning, shouting back at him from far off.

We were tired, so tired. My first-born brother and the man had to lift our grandfather from stone to stone where we found places to cross the rivers. Our grandmother is strong but her feet were bleeding. We could not carry the basket on our heads any longer, we couldn't carry anything except my little brother. We left our things under a bush. As long as our bodies get there, our grandmother said. Then we ate some wild fruit we didn't know from home and our stomachs ran. We were in the grass called elephant grass because it is nearly as tall as an elephant, that day we had those pains, and our grandfather couldn't just get down in front of people like my little brother, he went off into the grass to be on his own. We had to keep up, the man who led us always kept telling us, we must catch up, but we asked him to wait for our grandfather.

So everyone waited for our grandfather to catch up. But he didn't. It was the middle of the day; insects were singing in our ears and we couldn't hear him moving through the grass. We couldn't see him because the grass was so high and he was so small. But he must have been somewhere there inside his loose trousers and his shirt that was torn and our grandmother couldn't sew because she had no cotton. We knew he couldn't have gone far because he was weak and slow. We all went to look for him, but in groups, so we too wouldn't be hidden from each other in that grass. It got into our eyes and noses; we called him softly but the noise of the insects must have filled the little space left for hearing in his ears. We looked and looked but we couldn't find him. We stayed in that long grass all night. In my sleep I found him curled round in a place he had tramped down for himself, like the places we'd seen where the buck hide their babies.

When I woke up he still wasn't anywhere. So we looked again, and by now there were paths we'd made by going through the grass many times, it would be easy for him to find us if we couldn't find him. All that day we just sat and waited. Everything is very quiet when the sun is on your head, inside your head, even if you lie, like the animals, under the trees. I lay on my back and saw those ugly birds with hooked beaks and plucked necks flying round and round above us. We had passed them often where they were feeding on the bones of dead animals, nothing was ever left there for us to eat. Round and round, high up and then lower down and then high again. I saw their necks poking to this side and that. Flying round and round. I saw our grandmother, who sat up all the time with my little brother on her lap, was seeing them, too.

In the afternoon the man who led us came to our grandmother and told her the other people must move on. He said, If their children don't eat soon they will die.

Our grandmother said nothing.

I'll bring you water before we go, he told her.

Our grandmother looked at us, me, my first-born brother, and my little brother on her lap. We watched the other people getting up to leave. I didn't believe the grass would be empty, all around us, where they had been. That we would be alone in this place, the Kruger Park, the police or the animals would find us. Tears came out of my eyes and nose onto my hands but our grandmother took no notice. She got up, with her feet apart the way she puts them when she is going to lift firewood, at home in our village, she swung my little brother onto her back, tied him in her cloth-the top of her dress was torn and her big breasts were showing but there was nothing in them for him. She said, Come.

So we left the place with the long grass. Left behind. We went with the others and the man who led us. We started to go away, again.

There's a very big tent, bigger than a church or a school, tied down to the ground. I didn't understand that was what it would be, when we got there, away. I saw a thing like that the time our mother took us to the town because she heard our soldiers were there and she wanted to ask them if they knew where our father was. In that tent, people were praying and singing. This one is blue and white like that one but it's not for praying and singing, we live in it with other people who've come from our country. Sister from the clinic says we're two hundred without counting the babies, and we have new babies, some were born on the way through the Kruger Park.

Inside, even when the sun is bright it's dark and there's a kind of whole village in there. Instead of houses each family has a little place closed off with sacks or cardboard from boxes – whatever we can find – to show the other families it's yours and they shouldn't come in even though there's no door and no windows and no thatch, so that if you're standing up and you're not a small child you can see into everybody's house. Some people have even made paint from ground rocks and drawn designs on the sacks. **‖**

Of course, there really is a roof – the tent is the roof, far, high up. It's like a sky. It's like a mountain and we're inside it; through the cracks paths of dust lead down, so thick you think you could climb them. The tent keeps off the rain overhead but the water comes in at the sides and in the little streets between our places – you can only move along them one person at a time-the small kids like my little brother play in the mud. You have to step over them. My little brother doesn't play. Our grandmother takes him to the clinic when the doctor comes on Mondays. Sister says there's something wrong with his head, she thinks it's because we didn't have enough food at home. Because of the war. Because our father wasn't there. And then because he was so hungry in the Kruger Park. He likes just to lie about on our grandmother all day, on her lap or against her somewhere, and he looks at us and looks at us. He wants to ask something but you can see he can't. If I tickle him he may just smile. The clinic gives us special powder to make into porridge for him and perhaps one day he'll be all right.

When we arrived we were like him – my first-born brother and I. I can hardly remember. The people who live in the village near the tent took us to the clinic, it's where you have to sign that you've come – away, through the Kruger Park. We sat on the grass and everything was muddled. One Sister was pretty with her hair straightened and beautiful high-heeled shoes and she brought us the special powder. She said we must mix it with water and drink it slowly. We tore the packets open with our teeth and licked it all up, it stuck round my mouth and I sucked it from my lips and fingers. Some other children who had walked with us vomited. But I only felt everything in my belly moving, the stuff going down and around like a snake, and hiccups hurt me. Another Sister called us to stand in line on the verandah of the clinic but we couldn't. We sat all over the place there, falling against each other; the Sisters helped each of us up by the arm and then stuck a needle in it. Other needles drew our blood into tiny bottles. This was against sickness, but I didn't understand, every time my eyes dropped closed I thought I was walking, the grass was long, I saw the elephants, I didn't know we were away.

But our grandmother was still strong, she could still stand up, she knows how to write and she signed for us. Our grandmother got us this place in the tent against one of the sides, it's the best kind of place there because although the rain comes in, we can lift the flap when the weather is good and then the sun shines on us, the smells in the tent go out. Our grandmother knows a woman here who showed her where there is good grass for sleeping mats, and our grandmother made some for us. Once every month the food truck comes to the clinic. Our grandmother takes along one of the cards she signed and when it has been punched we get a sack of mealie meal. There are wheelbarrows to take it back to the tent; my first-born brother does this for her and then he and the other boys have races, steering the empty wheelbarrows back to the clinic. Sometimes he's lucky and a man who's bought beer in the village gives him money to deliver it – though that's not allowed, you're supposed to take that wheelbarrow straight back to the Sisters. He buys a cold drink and shares it with me if I catch him. On another day, every month, the church leaves a pile of old clothes in the clinic yard. Our grandmother has another card to get punched, and then we can choose something: I have two dresses, two pants and a jersey, so I can go to school.

The people in the village have let us join their school. I was surprised to find they speak our language; our grandmother told me, That's why they allow us to stay on their land. Long ago, in the time of our fathers, there was no fence that kills you, there was no Kruger Park between them and us, we were the same people under our own king, right from our village we left to this place we've come to.

Now that we've been in the tent so long – I have turned eleven and my little brother

183

is nearly three although he is so small, only his head is big, he's not come right in it yet – some people have dug up the bare ground around the tent and planted beans and mealies and cabbage. The old men weave branches to put up fences round their gardens. No one is allowed to look for work in the towns but some of the women have found work in the village and can buy things. Our grandmother, because she's still strong, finds work where people are building houses – in this village the people build nice houses with bricks and cement, not mud like we used to have at our home. Our grandmother carries bricks for these people and fetches baskets of stones on her head. And so she has money to buy sugar and tea and milk and soap. The store gave her a calendar she has hung up on our flap of the tent. I am clever at school and she collected advertising paper people throw away outside the store and covered my schoolbooks with it. She makes my first-born brother and me do our homework every afternoon before it gets dark because there is no room except to lie down, close together, just as we did in the Kruger Park, in our place in the tent, and candles are expensive. Our grandmother hasn't been able to buy herself a pair of shoes for church yet, but she has bought black school shoes and polish to clean them with for my first-born brother and me. Every morning, when people are getting up in the tent, the babies are crying, people are pushing each other at the taps outside and some children are already pulling the crusts of porridge off the pots we ate from last night, my first-born brother and I clean our shoes. Our grandmother makes us sit on our mats with our legs straight out so she can look carefully at our shoes to make sure we have done it properly. No other children in the tent have real school shoes. When we three look at them it's as if we are in a real house again, with no war, no away.

Some white people came to take photographs of our people living in the tent – they said they were making a film, I've never seen what that is though I know about it. A white woman squeezed into our space and asked our grandmother questions which were told to us in our language by someone who understands the white woman's.

How long have you been living like this?

She means here? our grandmother said. In this tent, two years and one month.

And what do you hope for the future?

Nothing. I'm here.

But for your children?

I want them to learn so that they can get good jobs and money.

Do you hope to go back to Mozambique – to your own country?

I will not go back.

But when the war is over – you won't be allowed to stay here? Don't you want to go home?

I didn't think our grandmother wanted to speak again. I didn't think she was going to answer the white woman. The white woman put her head on one side and smiled at us.

Our grandmother looked away from her and spoke – There is nothing. No home.

Why does our grandmother say that? Why? I'll go back. I'll go back through that Kruger Park. After the war, if there are no bandits any more, our mother may be waiting for us. And maybe when we left our grandfather, he was only left behind, he found his way somehow, slowly, through the Kruger Park, and he'll be there. They'll be home, and I'll remember them.

Nadine Gordimer: Telling Tales (ed Nadine Gordimer, 2005)

Touching the Void – Joe's Story

Two friends are climbing together. This is Joe's version of what happened next. Simon's point of view is on page 190.

Crouching down on my knees, I turned my back to the cliff edge and managed to get my axes to bite in deeply. Slowly, I lowered my legs over the cliff until the edge was against my stomach and I could kick my crampons into the ice wall below me. I felt them bite and hold. Removing one axe, I hammered it in again very close to the edge. It held fast and solid. I removed my ice hammer and lowered my chest and shoulders over the edge until I could see the ice wall and swing at it with the hammer. I was hanging on to the ice axe, reaching to my side to place the hammer solidly into the wall with my left hand. I got it to bite after a few blows but wasn't happy about it and removed it to try again. I wanted it to be perfect before I removed the axe embedded in the lip and lowered myself on to the hammer. As the hammer came out there was a sharp cracking sound and my right hand, gripping the axe, pulled down. The sudden jerk turned me outwards and instantly I was falling.

I hit the slope at the base of the cliff before I saw it coming. I was facing into the slope and both knees locked as I struck it. I felt a shattering blow in my knee, felt bones splitting, and screamed. The impact catapulted me over backwards and down the slope of the East Face. I slid, head-first, on my back. The rushing speed of it confused me. I thought of the drop below but felt nothing. Simon would be ripped off the mountain. He couldn't hold this. I screamed again as I jerked to a sudden violent stop.

Everything was still, silent. My thoughts raced madly. Then pain flooded down my thigh – a fierce burning fire coming down the inside of my thigh, seeming to ball in my groin, building and building until I cried out at it, and my breathing came in ragged gasps. My leg! Oh Jesus. My leg!

I hung, head down, on my back, left leg tangled in the rope above me and my right leg hanging slackly to one side. I lifted my head from the snow and stared, up across my chest, at a grotesque distortion in the right knee, twisting the leg into a strange zigzag. I didn't connect it with the pain which burnt my groin. That had nothing to do with my knee. I kicked my left leg free of the rope and swung round until I was hanging against the snow on my chest, feet down. The pain eased. I kicked my left foot into the slope and stood up.

A wave of nausea surged over me. I pressed my face into the snow, and the sharp cold seemed to calm me. Something terrible, something dark with dread occurred to me, and as I thought about it I felt the dark thought break into panic: 'I've broken my leg, that's it. I'm dead. Everyone said it ... if there's just two of you a broken ankle could turn into a death sentence ... if it's broken ... if... It doesn't hurt so much, maybe I've just ripped something.'

I kicked my right leg against the slope, feeling sure it wasn't broken. My knee exploded. Bone grated, and the fireball rushed from groin to knee. I screamed. I looked down at the knee and could see it was broken, yet I tried not to believe what I was seeing. It wasn't just broken, it was ruptured, twisted, crushed, and I could see the kink in the joint and knew what had happened. The impact had driven my lower leg up through the knee joint.

Oddly enough, looking at it seemed to help. I felt detached from it, as if I were making a clinical observation of someone else. I moved the knee gingerly, experimenting with it. I tried to bend it and stopped immediately, gasping at the rush of pain. When it moved I felt a grinding crunch; bone had moved, and a lot more besides. At least it wasn't an open fracture. I knew this as soon as I tried to move. I could feel no wetness, no blood. I reached down and caressed the knee with my right hand, trying to ignore the stabs of fire, so that I could feel it with enough force to be certain I wasn't bleeding. It was in one solid piece, but it felt huge, and twisted – and not mine. The pain kept flooding round it, pouring on fire, as if that might cure it then and there.

With a groan I squeezed my eyes tight shut. Hot tears filled my eyes and my contact lenses swam in them. I squeezed tight again and felt hot drops rolling over my face. It wasn't the pain, I felt sorry for myself, childishly so, and with that thought I couldn't help the tears. Dying had seemed so far away, and yet now everything was tinged with it. I shook my head to stop the tears, but the taint was still there.

I dug my axes into the snow, and pounded my good leg deeply into the soft slope until I felt sure it wouldn't slip. The effort brought back the nausea and I felt my head spin giddily to the point of fainting. I moved and a searing spasm of pain cleared away the faintness. I could see the summit of Seria Norte away to the west. I was not far below it. The sight drove home how desperately things had changed. We were above 19,000 feet, still on the ridge, and very much alone. I looked south at the small rise I had hoped to scale quickly and it seemed to grow with every second that I stared. I would never get over it. Simon would not be able to get me up it. He would leave me. He had no choice. I held my breath, thinking about it. Left here? Alone? I felt cold at the thought. I remembered Rob, who had been left to die... but Rob had been unconscious, had been dying. I had only a bad leg. Nothing to kill me. For an age I felt overwhelmed at the notion of being left; I felt like screaming, and I felt like swearing, but stayed silent. If I said a word I would panic. I could feel myself teetering on the edge of it. ▌▌

The rope which had been tight on my harness went slack. Simon was coming! He must know something had happened, I thought, but what shall I tell him? If I told him that I had only hurt my leg and not broken it, would that make him help me? My mind raced at the prospect of telling him that I was hurt. I pressed my face into the cold snow again and tried to think calmly. I had to cool it. If he saw me panicky and hysterical he might give up at once. I fought to stem my fears. Be rational about it, I thought. I felt myself calm down, and my breathing became steady; even the pain seemed tolerable.

'What happened? Are you okay?'

I looked up in surprise. I hadn't heard his approach. He stood at the top of the cliff looking down at me, puzzled. I made an effort to talk normally, as if nothing had happened:

'I fell. The edge gave way.' I paused, then I said as unemotionally as I could: 'I've broken my leg.'

His expression changed instantly. I could see a whole range of reactions in his face. I kept looking directly at him. I wanted to miss nothing.

'Are you sure it's broken?'

'Yes.'

He stared at me. It seemed that he looked harder and longer than he should have done because he turned away sharply. Not sharply enough though. I had seen the look come across his face briefly, but in that instant I knew his thoughts. He had an odd air of detachment. I felt unnerved by it, felt suddenly quite different from him, alienated. His eyes had been full of thoughts. Pity. Pity and something else; a distance given to a wounded animal which could not be helped. He had tried to hide it, but I had seen in, and I looked away full of dread and worry.

'I'll abseil down to you.'

He had his back to me, bending over a snow stake, digging down through the soft snow. He sounded matter-of-fact, and I wondered whether I was being unduly paranoid. I waited for him to say more, but he remained silent and I wondered what he was thinking. A short but very dangerous abseil from a poorly anchored snow stake put him down next to me quickly.

He stood close by me and said nothing. I had seen him glance at my leg but he made no comment. After some searching he found a packet of Paracetamols and handed me two pills. I swallowed them, and watched him trying to pull the abseil rope down. It refused to move. It had jammed in the snow bollard that he had dug around the snow stake above. Simon swore and set off towards the point where the wall was smallest, right on the crest of the ridge. I knew it was all unstable powder and so did he, but he had no choice. I looked away, unwilling to watch what I was sure would be a fatal fall down the West Face. Indirectly it would kill me as well, only a little more slowly.

Simon had said nothing about what he would do, and I had been nervous to prompt him. In an instant an uncrossable gap had come between us and we were no longer a team working together.

Joe Simpson: Touching the Void (2003)

Touching the Void – Simon's Story

Two friends are climbing together. This version is Joe's imagined account of Simon's point of view. Joe's version is on page 186. *(Strong language warning)*

Joe had disappeared behind a rise in the ridge and began moving faster than I could go. I was glad we had put the steep section behind us at last. I had felt so close to the end of everything on that ridge. Falling all the time and always on the very edge of the West Face. I felt tired and was grateful to be able to follow Joe's tracks instead of breaking trail.

I rested a while when I saw that Joe had stopped moving. Obviously he had found an obstacle and I thought I would wait until he started moving again. When the rope moved again I trudged forward after it, slowly.

Suddenly there was a sharp tug as the rope lashed out taut across the slope. I was pulled forward several feet as I pushed my axes into the snow and braced myself for another jerk. Nothing happened. I knew that Joe had fallen, but I couldn't see him, so I stayed put. I waited for about ten minutes until the tautened rope went slack on the snow and I felt sure that Joe had got his weight off me. I began to move along his footsteps cautiously, half expecting something else to happen. I kept tensed up and ready to dig my axes in at the first sign of trouble.

As I crested the rise, I could see down a slope to where the rope disappeared over the edge of a drop. I approached slowly, wondering what had happened. When I reached the top of the drop I saw Joe below me. He had one foot dug in and was leaning against the slope with his face buried in the snow. I asked him what had happened and he looked at me in surprise. I knew he was injured, but the significance didn't hit me at first.

He told me very calmly that he had broken his leg. He looked pathetic, and my immediate thought came without any emotion, You're fucked, matey. You're dead... no two ways about it! I think he knew it too. I could see it in his face. It was all totally rational. I knew where we were, I took in everything around me instantly, and knew he was dead. It never occurred to me that I might also die. I accepted without question that I could get off the mountain alone. I had no doubt about that.

I saw what Joe had tried to do and realised that, unless I could arrange an abseil, I would have to do the same. The snow at the top of the cliff was horrendous sugary stuff. I dug as much of the surface away as I could and then buried a snow stake in the mush I had uncovered. I felt sure it would never hold my weight so I started digging a wide snow bollard around the stake. When I finished I backed towards the cliff edge and tugged the rope. It held firm but I had no confidence in it. I thought of trying to back-climb the crest of the ridge where the cliff was smallest but decided it would be even more dangerous. I half-abseiled and half-climbed down the cliff, trying to get my weight off the rope. I felt it cutting through the bollard. It held firm.

When I reached the foot of the cliff I saw that Joe's leg was in a bad way and that he was suffering. He seemed calm but had a sort of hunted, fearful look in his eyes. He knew the score as well as I did. I gave him some pills for the pain but knew they were not strong enough to help much. His leg was twisted and misshapen at the knee joint, and I thought that if I could see that through his thick polar-fibre trousers then it must be really bad.

I was at a loss for something to say. The change in our fortunes was too abrupt. I found that the ropes had jammed and knew I would have to go back up, alone, to free them. In a way, it took my mind off things, and gave me time to settle into the new situation. I had to solo back up the cliff, and the only way was right on the crest of the ridge. I was frightened of attempting it. Joe tried moving beside me and very nearly fell off. I grabbed him and put him back into balance. He stayed silent. He had unroped so I had been able to arrange the abseil and I think he was quiet because he knew that if I hadn't grabbed him he would have fallen the length of the East Face. I left him then, and forgot about him.

The climb up the edge of the cliff was the hardest and most dangerous thing I'd ever done. Several times my leg broke through the powder into space. When I was half-way up I realised I couldn't go back, but I didn't think I would get up it. I seemed to be climbing on nothing. Everything I touched simply broke away. Every step either sank back, collapsed or crumbled down the West Face, but incredibly I seemed to be gaining height. I don't know how long it took. It felt like hours. When eventually I pulled myself on to the slope above I was shaking and so strung out that I had to stop still and calm myself.

I looked back and was amazed to see that Joe had started traversing away from the cliff. He was trying to help himself by contouring round the small rise in front of him. He moved so slowly, planting his axes in deeply until his arms were buried and then making a frightening little hop sideways. He shuffled across the slope, head down, completely enclosed in his own private struggle. Below him I could see thousands of feet of open face falling into the eastern glacier bay. I watched him quite dispassionately. I couldn't help him, and it occurred to me that in all likelihood he would fall to his death. I wasn't disturbed by the thought. In a way I hoped he would fall. I knew I couldn't leave him while he was still fighting for it, but I had no idea how I might help him. I could get down. If I tried to get him down I might die with him. It didn't frighten me. It just seemed a waste. It would be pointless. I kept staring at him expecting him to fall...

After a long wait I turned and went up to the snow stake. I rearranged the stake and then backed down to the cliff edge again. I prayed it would hold me, and when I touched down on the slope below prayed again that it wouldn't jam. I had no intention of repeating the climb up the crest. The rope slid down easily and I turned with it, half-expecting to see that Joe had gone. He was still climbing away from me. In all the time it had taken me to get up and down he had covered only 100 feet. I started after him.

Joe Simpson: Touching the Void (2003)

Touching the Void
Activities

I Fell Through Arctic Ice

Before Reading

■ Read the extract below. With a partner, annotate the extract with as many questions as you can.

> Frantic, I ripped off my mittens. Trying to save my dogs, I was prepared to lose my hands to savage cold. It wasn't enough.

The final line of this text is:

> 'It's time to live again.'

■ Work on your own. Based on the title, 'I Fell Through Arctic Ice', the extract above, and the last line, come up with some adjectives that you think might describe the text you are going to read, for example, 'sad'.

■ Make a list of your adjectives as a class.

After Reading

Your Response

■ Think to yourself for a moment about your response to the text. What did it make you think or feel? Share your thoughts with the person next to you.

■ As a class, cross off any adjectives on your list that do not seem to describe the text. Discuss what other adjectives should be added to the list now you have read the whole text.

■ With a partner choose three adjectives from the class list which you think best sum up the whole article. Be prepared to point to particular sections of the text to support your choice of adjectives.

■ Compare your choices as a class.

—————————— Your Own Writing ——————————

■ You are going to do a piece of your own writing based on some of the work you have done on 'I Fell Through Arctic Ice'. You could write a fictional story or write about a real experience.

■ Choose three adjectives from the class list you developed for 'I Fell Through Arctic Ice'. Brainstorm some ideas around each one. Choose your best ideas to develop into a short piece of writing.

■ Your piece of writing must contain the following sentences from the text:

'Alone it's always dangerous'

'This is a last resort'

'So what now?'

How to Survive When Lost in the Mountains

Before Reading

Predictions

■ As a class, brainstorm your predictions about the text from the title: 'How to Survive When Lost in the Mountains', including what kind of text you think it might be.

After Reading

Audience for a Bestseller

1. Instruction writing?

■ Remind yourself of the predictions you made from the title. How closely does the text match your predictions?

One of your predictions was probably that this would be a piece of instruction writing aimed at helping mountaineers survive when lost and that is what the text seems to do. However, unlike most instruction writing, some of the information included is not really necessary for someone to be able to follow the instructions. Imagine you are going to edit the text to cut any information that is not absolutely necessary.

■ With a partner, decide what you would cut, if possible by crossing out these sections on a photocopy of the text. Remember that the illustration is part of the text.

■ Look again at the sections you decided were not necessary to the instructions. Why do you think they have been included?

2. Why did people buy the book?

The text comes from a book called *The Worst Case Scenario Survival Handbook*. Other entries include how to survive an attack by killer bees and how to jump from a moving vehicle. The book is a worldwide bestseller. Is there really a big audience of people who need instructions for such a wide range of adventures? Read some the extracts on page 196 which are from reviews of the book for the Amazon website. As you read, notice the reasons people give for buying the book.

Amazon reader reviews

> How to fend off a shark attack? How to jump from a five story building into a dumpster? How to survive a hostage situation? I have to ask myself...who in the world (outside the Navy SEALS) needs to KNOW this stuff? Well, heck, not me. But I LOVED reading this book...

> ... it just might be possible that I'll need know how to treat frostbite, survive at sea, use a defibrillator to start someone's heart, survive an earthquake, make a fire without matches or avoid being struck by lightening. Now I know – and maybe one of the important things I know is that you CAN survive from some pretty awful things!

> Most of us daydream occasionally about a life with more excitement and adventure...

> Hopefully, no one reading this book will ever have to actually use it. In spite of the scare factor, however (or perhaps because of it), this is one VERY interesting, fascinating, funny book, and great for passing around at parties. It has a 'you have GOT to be kidding me' factor that is just fantastic.

> I'm impressed with this book. Irony of ironies, I read this book the day before the 6.8 earthquake here in Seattle. How did the section on 'How to Survive an Earthquake' fare? Pretty well.

■ As a class, discuss what you have discovered about the audience and purpose of 'How to Survive When Lost in the Mountains'. Would you still say it was instruction writing for an audience of mountaineers?

Your Own Writing

The Blurb

■ Write a blurb for the book *The Worst Case Scenario Survival Handbook*. Bear in mind the work you have done on the audience and purpose of the book in the activity 'Audience for a Bestseller'. Try to write your blurb so that it will appeal to these readers. You can use the information below, taken from the Amazon website, to help you if you wish.

- The book is being marketed as a humorous title.

- Some of the sections include: landing a plane, jumping from a motorcycle to a moving car, winning a swordfight.

- The information contained in *The Worst-Case Scenario Survival Handbook* is all quite sound. Authors Joshua Piven and David Borgenicht consulted numerous experts in their fields (they're mentioned at the end of the book) to discover how to survive various awful events. Parachute doesn't open? Your best bet for survival is to hook your arms through the straps of a fellow jumper's chute – and even then you're likely to dislocate both shoulders and break both legs. Car sinking in water? Open the window immediately to equalize pressure, then open the car door and swim to the surface. Buried in an avalanche? Spit on the snow – it will tell you which direction is really up. Then dig as fast as you can.

- Each survival skill is explained in simple steps with helpful illustrations.

Your Own Worst Case Scenario

■ Write another entry for the book, giving your own advice on how to survive. You could choose from one of the scenarios below, or make up one of your own. Your entry can be funny or serious but should include some helpful instructions combined with some interesting information.

- How to survive a weekend with no money to spend.

- How to survive without television.

- How to survive a boring lesson.

- How to survive a family holiday.

The Ultimate Safari

───── Before Reading ─────

African Adventure

> **The African Adventure Lives On.**
> **You can do it!**
> **The ultimate safari or expedition with leaders who know Africa.**

A safari is a holiday where you see, or sometimes hunt, animals in their natural habitat. These holidays are usually in Africa and involve travelling in national parks, riding in Land Rovers and staying in tents.

- ■ As a class, discuss who you think might respond to the advert, and what they would be expecting from the trip.

Looking at an Extract

- ■ In small groups, take one of the extracts below. In your group, come up with as many 'who, what, where, why, when and how' questions as you can.

- ■ As a class, collect your questions and keep a record of them where you can see them as you read. Look out for as many answers as you can.

> That night my mother went to the shop and she didn't come back. Ever.

> When the sun was going down our grandmother and grandfather came.

> So they decided ...we would go away. We children were pleased.

> I said Gogo how will you go to church now even without shoes, but she said we had a long journey and too much to carry.

> At that village we met other people who were also going away. We joined then because they seemed to know better than we did where that was.

> The only food we could eat was what the baboons ate, dry little figs full of ants that grow along the branches of the trees at the river. It was hard to be like the animals.

> They can give us food from the dustbins, she said, she started wailing and our grandmother had to grab her and put a hand over her mouth.

During Reading

'It was hard to be like the animals.'

■ Read as far as 'It was hard to be like the animals.' **II**

Comparisons

The narrator often describes things by comparing them with things or people from her village. Some examples are given below.

> I've seen that sign of a head without eyes or skin or hair on an iron box at the mission hospital we used to have before it was blown up.

> The almost grown-up ones wrestled like my first-born brother with his friends – only they used trunks instead of arms.

> The warthogs stopped dead, when they heard us, and swerved off the way a boy in our village used to zigzag on the bicycle his father had brought back from the mines.

■ You are now going to discuss why you think Nadine Gordimer makes these comparisons. With a partner, look at the possible reasons given below. Discuss which statements you agree with, or come up with an explanation of your own.

– Having the narrator refer back to her village all the time reminds the reader that this is the most important place in the world for her.

– Gordimer wants to show that the narrator hasn't experienced much of the world so she can only make sense of what is happening by comparing it to the things in her village.

– The narrator is worried she will forget all about her home so she keeps referring back to it.

– Having the narrator refer back to her village all the time reminds the reader that she has lost her home.

– The narrator is glad to leave her village – the comparisons show that it wasn't a nice place to be.

'...they had only seen animals.'

■ Read as far as '...they had only seen animals.' **II**

■ As a class, share any answers you have found in the text to the list of questions you came up with.

■ Continue to look for answers to your remaining questions until you have read the whole story.

'Some people have even made paint from ground rocks'

■ Read as far as 'Some people have even made paint from ground rocks.' **II**

■ How have people tried to make their homes in the big tent? Why do you think this might be important?

———————— After Reading ————————

Questions Answered?

■ As a class, look back at the questions you asked of the extracts you looked at before reading the story. Can you answer all of them now? Discuss which questions remain unanswered and why you think they remain unanswered.

Your Response

■ Think to yourself for a moment about your response to the text. What did it make you think or feel? With a partner discuss your reactions to the story.

■ Write a few sentences explaining how you responded to the story. Use one or more of the words below or use words or phrases of your own.

sad	hopeful	angry	admiring	sympathetic	disappointed
depressed	optimistic	pessimistic	frightened	thoughtful	relieved

The Ultimate Safari

The family in the story are victims of the civil war in their country, Mozambique, in Africa. Like many other refugees they flee across Kruger National Park, probably to Zimbabwe.

■ In pairs, discuss why you think Nadine Gordimer called this story 'The Ultimate Safari' and why an advert for a holiday appears at the beginning.

■ In role as the writer, write an introduction to the story, explaining why you chose the title and why you started the story with the advert.

Touching the Void – Joe's story

Before Reading

> **A Dilemma**
>
> You are climbing in some remote and dangerous mountains with your friend, Joe. Joe breaks his leg in a fall and as a result is barely able to move. You have no way of contacting anyone for help unless you climb back down to base camp. You suspect that Joe will not last long enough for you to make the journey. If you stay with him you are at risk yourself as it is extremely cold and you do not have enough food for more than a few days.

What Could You Do?

- With a partner, list as many possible options as you can. Now draw a chart like the one below and fill it in for the different choices you could make.

Choice	Possible consequences	How likely I would be to take this option

During Reading

'I could feel myself teetering on the edge of it.'

- Read as far as 'I could feel myself teetering on the edge of it.' **II**

- Simon climbs down to Joe. With a partner, role play the conversation you think Simon and Joe might have when he sees what has happened.

- Watch some of the role plays as a class and discuss some of the different ideas you had about how Simon might react.

- Read to the end of the piece.

─────────────── **After Reading** ───────────────

Your Response

■ Think to yourself for a moment about your response to the text. What did it make you think or feel? Share your thoughts with the person sitting next to you.

─────────────── **Your Own Writing** ───────────────

'The impact had driven my lower leg up through the knee joint'

■ Re-read the text as far as 'The impact had driven my lower leg up through the knee joint.' **II**

Writing a Paragraph about the Text

Joe Simpson describes the breaking of his leg in several different ways.

■ On your own, choose a phrase or a section that really helped you to imagine the accident.

■ Write a paragraph explaining how Joe Simpson has used language effectively in this section. Your paragraph should include a topic sentence, evidence and some development.

1. Topic sentence

■ The first sentence in your paragraph should explain how Simpson used language effectively. For example:

Simpson describes not just the physical pain in his leg but lets you know how he is feeling as well.

2. Evidence

■ Use a quotation or example from the text that backs up the point you made in your topic sentence. An example means that you refer to a particular bit of the text in your own words, without actually quoting. For example:

Simpson describes not just the physical pain in his leg but lets you know how he is feeling as well, saying to himself 'I've broken my leg, that's it. I'm dead.'

3. Development

■ This part of your paragraph is very important as it is where you take your ideas further. If you are writing for a test or exam, this part of the paragraph will help you to get good marks. To take your ideas further you could do one or more of the following:

– Explain how your evidence backs up the point in your topic sentence. For example:

Simpson describes not just the physical pain in his leg but lets you know how he is feeling as well, saying to himself 'I've broken my leg, that's it. I'm dead.' In telling the reader his thoughts he shows that the pain is the least of his worries and that he understands straight away how serious the accident is.

– Develop the idea in your topic sentence in more detail. For example:

Simpson describes not just the physical pain in his leg but lets you know how he is feeling as well, saying to himself 'I've broken my leg, that's it. I'm dead.' Giving his inner thoughts and feelings draws the reader in and creates sympathy for the terrible situation he is in, especially as it is told in the first person.

– Make a comment on the way the writer has used language in the evidence you used. For example:

Simpson describes not just the physical pain in his leg but lets you know how he is feeling as well, saying to himself 'I've broken my leg, that's it. I'm dead.' The way he writes this terrifying thought in two very short sentences has a dramatic impact.

– Give your personal response. For example:

Simpson describes not just the physical pain in his leg but lets you know how he is feeling as well, saying to himself 'I've broken my leg, that's it. I'm dead.' I hadn't even thought about this aspect of the accident. I was only thinking about the physical pain but this reminded me that they can't just call an ambulance, they are on the side of a mountain, alone, and it made me tense and worried for him.

Simon's Feelings

■ As a class, discuss how Simon might have been feeling at the points that follow:

> Simon was coming! He must know something had happened, I thought, but what shall I tell him?

> 'What happened? Are you okay?'

> I looked up in surprise. I hadn't heard his approach. He stood at the top of the cliff looking down at me, puzzled. I made an effort to talk normally as if nothing had happened.

> His expression changed instantly. I could see a whole range of reactions in his face. I kept looking directly at him. I wanted to miss nothing.

> 'Are you sure it's broken?'

> His eyes had been full of thoughts. Pity. Pity and something else; a distance given to a wounded animal which could not be helped.

> Simon had said nothing about what he would do, and I had been nervous to prompt him. In an instant an uncrossable gap had come between us and we were no longer a team working together.

■ What clues do Joe and the reader get about what Simon is thinking?

■ On your own, go back to the 'Before Reading' activity on Simon's dilemma. Which option do you think Simon is going to take and why? Support your answer with evidence from the text.

Touching the Void – Simon's Story

In order to do this work you will need to have read 'Touching the Void – Joe's Story' (page 186).

————— Before Reading —————

A Mile in His Shoes

Simon's story was also written by Joe Simpson, imagining what things were like from his friend's perspective. Simon has since told Joe that his version is pretty true to what Simon actually thought and felt.

There is an American saying 'Don't judge a man until you have walked a mile in his shoes.'

- With a partner discuss what you think this saying means.

- Why do you think Joe might have chosen to 'walk in Simon's shoes' by writing his side of the story?

————— After Reading —————

Similarities and Differences

Joe Simpson wrote both versions of the accident. In the second one he tried to tell it from the point of view of his friend, Simon.

- With a partner discuss how Joe Simpson gives the impression that Simon is telling this part of the story himself.

- Share your ideas as a class.

Working with More than One Text

Openings and Endings 1

For this work you will need to have read at least three of the texts in this section.

- Re-read the openings and the endings of the texts you have read from the selection reproduced at the end of this activity. (*NB: The opening and ending to Touching the Void is the chapter included in this anthology, not the whole text.*)

- In a group of four, choose one of the texts you have read. Two of you should discuss the opening and two of you the ending. Use the questions below to help you to get your discussion started.

    - Is this written in the first or third person? Present tense or past tense? What difference does this make to the reader?

    - What do you notice about the length of the sentences? Have any very long or very short sentences been used? Why?

    - What else do you notice about the way the writer has used language, for example surprising or interesting words, phrases or descriptions?

- Now get together again as a four. Read aloud the opening and the ending to each other.

- Discuss the opening and ending as a four using the questions below to get your discussion started.

    - When you read the ending, do you notice any repetition, or echoing of ideas or use of language from the opening?

    - What has developed about the ideas or argument through the piece?

    - What effect is the writer trying to achieve with this opening? How does she or he try to get you to read on?

    - What effect is the writer trying to achieve with this ending? Any final message or viewpoint?

    - What do you like about this opening and ending? Why?

- As a class, make a list of some features of good openings and endings.

The Openings

I have travelled 11,000 Arctic miles with dogs, summer and winter. They've been my life. There are fewer than 300 purebred Canadian Eskimo dogs left in the world and I had 15 of them. I sank all my love and money into those dogs, proud to keep the breed's working talents alive. I learnt from the best, guys who in the 1980s had crossed Antarctica and made it to the North Pole with dogs, perfectionists who knew all there was to know. I watched, listened, kept my mouth shut, and one day decided to go it alone. It felt a natural progression.

The number one cause of death when lost in the mountains is hypothermia – humans are basically tropical animals. Staying calm in the face of darkness, loneliness, and the unknown will greatly increase your chances of survival. Eighty percent of mountain survival is your reaction to fear, 10 percent is your survival gear, and the other 10 percent is knowing how to use it. Always tell someone else where you are going and when you will return.

The African Adventure Lives On…You can do it!
The ultimate safari or expedition
With leaders who know Africa.
Travel Advertisement, Observer, London, 27/11/88

That night our mother went to the shop and she didn't come back. Ever. What happened? I don't know. My father also had gone away one day and never come back; but he was fighting in the war. We were in the war, too, but we were children, we were like our grandmother and grandfather, we didn't have guns. The people my father was fighting – the bandits, they are called by our government - ran all over the place and we ran away from them like chickens chased by dogs. We didn't know where to go.

Crouching down on my knees, I turned my back to the cliff edge and managed to get my axes to bite in deeply. Slowly, I lowered my legs over the cliff until the edge was against my stomach and I could kick my crampons into the ice wall below me. I felt them bite and hold. Removing one axe, I hammered it in again very close to the edge. It held fast and solid. I removed my ice hammer and lowered my chest and shoulders over the edge until I could see the ice wall and swing at it with the hammer. I was hanging on to the ice axe, reaching to my side to place the hammer solidly into the wall with my left hand. I got it to bite after a few blows but wasn't happy about it and removed it to try again. I wanted it to be perfect before I removed the axe embedded in the lip and lowered myself on to the hammer. As the hammer came out there was a sharp cracking sound and my right hand, gripping the axe, pulled down. The sudden jerk turned me outwards and instantly I was falling.

The Endings

So what now? My dogs and I were inseparable; I miss them desperately. All I want is dog hairs on my clothes again. The plan is a move to Greenland. It's time to live again.

FOOD. Pack carbohydrates: bagels, trail mix, granola bars, and so on. Proteins need heat to break down and require more water for digestion.

Why does our grandmother say that? Why? I'll go back. I'll go back through that Kruger Park. After the war, if there are no bandits any more, our mother may be waiting for us. And maybe when we left our grandfather, he was only left behind, he found his way somehow, slowly, through the Kruger Park, and he'll be there. They'll be home, and I'll remember them.

Simon had said nothing about what he would do, and I had been nervous to prompt him. In an instant an uncrossable gap had come between us and we were no longer a team working together.

Your Own Writing

Openings and Endings 2

■ Remember (or invent) an experience you have had in which you experienced physical hardship, or had a bit of an adventure.

■ Write two openings and two endings to your adventure, using some of the features of good openings and endings you have discussed as a class.

■ Read some of your passages aloud to the class. After each reading, discuss what you liked about the opening and ending, and whether you noticed the writer using any of the features you discussed.

Extension Work

Openings and Endings 3 – The Whole Adventure

■ Choose one paired opening and ending to develop into a piece of writing about an adventure story. You could use someone else's opening and ending if you prefer. Your writing can be fiction or non-fiction.

A Question of Sport

My Heroes Were Olympians

The text you are going to read is a speech made by Sebastian Coe to persuade the International Olympic Committee to allow Britain to host the 2012 Olympics in London. His speech was one of several which made up the London 'bid'.

Mr President, Mr Honorary Life President, Members of the International Olympic Committee

I stand here today because of the inspiration of the Olympic Movement.

When I was 12 about the same age as Amber I was marched into a large school hall with my classmates. We sat in front of an ancient, black and white TV and watched grainy pictures from the Mexico Olympic Games.

Two athletes from our home town were competing. John Sherwood won a bronze medal in the 400m hurdles. His wife Sheila just narrowly missed gold in the long jump.

That day a window to a new world opened for me.

By the time I was back in my classroom, I knew what I wanted to do and what I wanted to be.

The following week I stood in line for hours at my local track just to catch a glimpse of the medals the Sherwoods had brought home.

It didn't stop there. Two days later I joined their club.

Two years later Sheila gave me my first pair of racing spikes. 35 years on, I stand before you with those memories still fresh. Still inspired by this great Movement.

My journey here to Singapore started in that school hall and continues today in wonder and in gratitude. Gratitude that those flickering images of the Sherwoods, and Wolde, Gammoudi, Doubell and Hines drew me to a life in that most potent celebration of humanity Olympic sport. And that gratitude drives me and my team to do whatever we can to inspire young people to choose sport. Whoever they are, wherever they live and whatever they believe.

Today that task is so much harder.

Today's children live in a world of conflicting messages and competing distractions. Their landscape is cluttered. Their path to Olympic sport is often obscured. But it's a world we must understand and must respond to.

My heroes were Olympians.

My children's heroes change by the month.

And they are the lucky ones. Millions more face the obstacle of limited resources and the resulting lack of guiding role models.

In my travels over the last two years, speaking with many of you, I've had many conversations about how we meet this challenge. And I've been reassured and I've been uplifted. We share a common goal for the future of sport.

No group of leaders does more than you to engage the hearts and minds of young people.

But every year the challenge of bringing them to Olympic sport becomes tougher.

The choice of Host City is the most powerful means you have to meet this challenge. But it takes more than 17 days of superb Olympic competition. It takes a broader vision. And the global voice to communicate that vision over the full four years of the Olympiad.

Today in Britain's fourth bid in recent years we offer London's vision of inspiration and legacy.

Choose London today and you send a clear message to the youth of the world: more than ever, the Olympic Games are for you.

Mr President, Members of the IOC.

Some might say that your decision today is between five similar bids. That would be to undervalue the opportunity before you.

In the past, you have made bold decisions. Decisions which have taken the Movement forward in new and exciting directions.

Your decision today is critical.

It is a decision about which bid offers the vision and sporting legacy to best promote the Olympic cause. It is a decision about which city will help us show a new generation why sport matters. In a world of many distractions, why Olympic sport matters. And in the 21st century why the Olympic Ideals still matter so much.

On behalf of the youth of today, the athletes of tomorrow and the Olympians of the future, we humbly submit the bid of London 2012.

Sebastian Coe (2005)

The person who coached Sebastian Coe in delivering the speech gives his comments on page 212.

The Voice Coach

The person who coached Sebastian Coe in delivering his Olympic bid speech (see page 210) outlines the advice he gave.

On Wednesday 6th July, 2005 at 12.49pm British Standard Time the International Olympic Committee president Jacques Rogge made the long-awaited announcement that London had been chosen above four other competing cities to host the 2012 Olympic Games. Representatives of the bid teams from London, New York, Moscow; Madrid and Paris had gathered in Singapore that morning to make a final 45-minute appeal to the IOC members. This was followed by a series of voting rounds conducted via electronic ballot. In the last of these Paris and London were the only cities still in contention. London's victory was secured in the end by the slimmest of margins – just four votes.

That morning the London team was led by Sebastian (Seb) Coe twice an Olympic gold medal winner in the 1500 meters (1980 and 1984) and a former Conservative MP who in 1997 became private secretary to Conservative Party leader William Hague. Coe was just one among several speakers on behalf of the London cause. In the 45 minutes allotted each bid team, a series of people were expected to cover some 18 IOC themes including everything from the sporting history and heritage of each city to the nitty-gritty plans to provide the necessary transport systems needed to cope during the Olympics. In the end, commentators were convinced that Coe's passionate and unexpectedly personal speech played a decisive role in London's victory. The BBC described his approach as a 'masterstroke'

Before flying out to Singapore, Coe and the rest of the London bid team received specialist voice coaching from Master of Voice, Stewart Pearce, who here shares some of his insights concerning the speech.

Since 1980 I have been a professional voice coach, coaching famous actors, teaching at leading Drama Schools and supporting production work with numerous theatre companies. I also coach 'corporate clients' – people in leading businesses who want to improve the impact of their voices when speaking in public. In 2005 I was invited to help Seb Coe and other members of the London Olympic bid team; those that were due to speak to the IOC through the stages of the 2012 bid process, and then finally in Singapore.

The London bid was blessed in having Seb Coe as its Chair. He was one of this country's most famous athletes, as well as being very knowledgeable about the Olympic Games. Seb had been an MP and in 1997 become private secretary to the Conservative Party leader William Hague – one of the best speakers in the House of Commons. Seb Coe knew what great public speaking could be.

This combined expertise (athlete and politician) gave him a considerable edge over the other bidding speakers. Not only was he able to express the important messages the IOC wanted to hear, but in addition he was in a position to provide an entirely credible personal account of the impact the Olympic Games had had on his own successful sporting career.

A key part of understanding the impact Seb's speech had in Singapore is recognising how it must have stood out from the background of the many technical details the IOC members were to listen to on the Final day. How refreshing it must have been to hear Seb's childhood memories.

I believe by explaining the importance of the Olympics through his own personal development as an athlete, Seb Coe provided the perfect foundation for the central part of the speech concerning the legacy the London Olympics would leave for future generations of sportsmen and women. The Olympic Games potential to cut through all the fads and celebrity distractions that compete for young people's attention was similar to the power that captured Seb's imagination, and set him on the path to international athletic success.

Of course, a speech is not just about logical structure and well-written phrases. Ideally it needs to fit the speaker's personal rhythms – and this is something I wanted to ensure Seb's delivery managed to achieve. It had to be spoken with a magnetic conviction, and a rhythm that was true to Seb, capturing his spirit and essence. This may sound hard to understand, but imagine this speech being delivered like a railway platform announcement and then you may be able to understand how the most special of words can fail to have an impact.

People are often out of touch with the potential in their bodies to sound words in ways that give them great resonance and profundity; in ways that put them in touch with their deeper, and more truthful selves. Without such power words cannot touch other people's hearts, for sound is a key dimension of a word's meaning.

When we speak we always have enough breath with which to express a thought, and ensuring that the speech fitted with Seb's breathing patterns was one of the tasks tackled. In the coaching situation we also reviewed words or phrases that could be enriched to act as 'hooks' to draw in the IOC listeners. By 'enriched', I mean that the words were to be 'sounded' with sincerity, depth and profundity.

For example, take the second and third paragraphs; the opening: 'When I was 12...' naturally invites a fairly quick and rising note, then the tone needs to drop and resonate far more deeply on the words 'ancient', 'black and white'; and 'grainy'. Similarly, 'Two athletes from our home town were competing...' invites a more abrupt rising sound while the words 'John Sherwood won a bronze medal...' and 'his wife Sheila just narrowly missed gold...' need to come from a deeper more profound place.

In these simple ways the ideas were transformed into profound memories. He was able to help the IOC share in the experiences and so they understood the importance of what that day in Singapore was about. He persuaded the IOC that their decision was not just about a one-off sporting event, but that it could be a potential catalyst for a new generation of 21st Century athletes – a catalyst that London was best placed to prove. And of course they agreed.

Stewart Pearce (2007)

Chin Up, My Little Angel – Winning is for Losers

My eldest daughter is not sleek. In fact, to be brutally honest she has the aerodynamic properties of a bungalow and the coordination of an American bombing raid.

She puts a huge effort into running. Her arms and legs flail around like the Flying Scotsman's pistons but despite this you need a theodolite[1] to ascertain that she is actually moving forwards. She's a bit of a duffer at the school's sports day.

Luckily, the school tries to operate a strict 'no competition' rule. The game starts, children exert energy and then the game finishes. This doesn't work terribly well with the 50-metre running race but often there are never any winners and consequently there are never any losers.

That's the theory, but round the edge of the sports ground there's a communal picnic for parents. I had been asked to bring along a potato salad, which sounds simple enough but oh no. My potato salad was going to be creamier and made with higher-quality potatoes than anyone else's potato salad. This is why I got up at 4.30 a.m. to make it.

Nobody was going to scoop my potato salad quietly into the bushes. Nobody was going to make joke retching noises behind my back. I was out there to win, to crush the competition like beetles.

My daughter did not understand. 'You told me it doesn't matter if I come last in the race,' she said.

'It doesn't,' I replied.

'So why,' she pressed on, 'are you trying to win a competition for potato salads when there isn't one?'

There bloody well was. And a competition for pasta salads, too. And quiche. But all of these paled alongside the brownie wars.

[1] *Theodolite = a surveying instrument for measuring angles*

Obviously, I chose the ones made by my wife but pretty soon I was surrounded by a gaggle of women. 'Try mine,' they said. 'Try mine.' It was just like the old days when schools had teams and competition and everyone crowded round shouting: 'Pick me, pick me.'

I was never picked. I was always left at the back like the spring onion in the bottom of the fridge: 'Oh do we have to have Clarkson, sir? He's useless.'

I was therefore determined that no brownie should be left out, but this wasn't enough. I was being pushed to decide, publicly, whose was best: my wife's with the creamy centre; the ones made with chocolate that had been specially imported from America; or the ones with pecans floating in the middle. 'They were all lovely,' I said, sticking to the spirit of the day.

What spirit? What's the point of protecting children from the horror of failure on the sports pitch when their parents are all giving one another Chinese burns on the touchline? 'My brownies are better than yours. Say it! Say it!'

I spoke last night to a man who bunged one of the teachers 50 quid at his daughter's sports day, saying:

'Look, if it's close for first and second, you know what to do.'

The following year his daughter wrote to him saying: 'Dear Dad, please let me come where I come. Don't try to bribe anyone.' He did as asked and she came in second. But he wasn't finished. He took the cup she won to the engravers and had it inscribed with a big '1st'.

It's not as if children don't understand the concept of losing. Mine regularly have their stomachs blown open by aliens or their heads kicked in by a Russian agent.

Of course, you could be good parents and turn up at sports day with a bowl of tinned prunes. You could force your children to put the PlayStation away and stick to Monopoly, which has no winners and losers because nobody in the whole of human history has ever had the patience to finish a game.

Think about it. If your child has no understanding of failure, how will he cope when he walks round the back of the bike sheds one day to find his girlfriend in a passionate embrace with Miggins Major? There'll be a bloodbath.

I don't want my children to be unhappy. Ever. It broke my heart when, as predicted, Emily was last in her running race, thumping across the line like a buffalo. I couldn't bear to watch her fighting back the tears of humiliation.

But what do you do? Well, why not teach them that losing is better than winning. Certainly, it's impossible to make someone laugh if you've come home first. 'So anyway, I got the deal, won the lottery and woke up in bed the next day with Cameron Diaz and Claudia Schiffer.' That's nice but it's not funny.

Furthermore, arranging your face when you win is impossible. You have to look proud but magnanimous and that's hard even for Dustin Hoffman. Michael Schumacher has been winning since he was eight and he still can't pull it off.

All the funniest people in life are abject and total failures. There's no such thing as a funny supermodel or a successful businessman who causes your sides to split every time he opens his mouth.

This is presumably why I felt a certain sense of pride as we trudged home from the sports day picnic. Everyone else was carrying empty bowls that had been licked clean. And me? Well, my bowl was still full of uneaten potato salad.

And I got a column out of it.

Jeremy Clarkson: The World According to Clarkson (2005),
originally published as a column in The Sunday Times (2002)

Tournament

Matthew Polly went to the Shaolin Temple in China, famous as the birthplace of both Zen Buddhism and kung fu. After training for two years, he was considered ready to represent the Temple at the Zhengszhou tournament, a big Chinese kickboxing competition.

I was laughing. I was buoyant. I was literally bouncing down the hallway. What was this? Nothing. A kickboxing match? Nothing. Where was the challenge in this? Send me into a real battle. A reckless courage pumped my veins. I was ready to defend the Ardennes, charge the Turkish lines at Gallipoli, hold the pass at Thermopylae[1]. My heart grappled with my brain to see which was bigger as my ego shouted encouragement from the sidelines. Coach Cheng, who'd seen this fever in other fighters before, gripped my shoulder to make certain I didn't crack.

I went up and stood next to the Champ, who was waiting at the edge of the arena.

'You fought well yesterday,' I said.

'So did you.'

We fell into silence. I felt awkward, but not because we were about to climb onto a platform and start fighting. I felt awkward because I liked him and we were about to climb onto a platform and start fighting. In all my previous matches, there was something that irritated me or that I didn't respect about my opponent, but I liked the Champ. He was *laoshi*[2]. There was no bullshit about him. He was just one of those solid, straightforward peasant kids who came to Shaolin from his parents' farm and had trained really hard for the last decade and was now the best in the world at what he did. And while there was no way for me to know for certain, I was pretty sure he liked me, too.

'*Wo ju ni chenggong,*' I said. 'I wish you success.'

It is what everyone says to a fighter before a match, everyone but his opponent, of course, because he'd be wishing for his own defeat.

[1] *Three famous battles with heavy losses*
[2] *Laoshi = respected teacher*

It took the Champ a moment, his brow furrowed, before he got the joke and smiled.

'No, no, no,' he replied, 'I wish you success.'

'No, no, no, I wish you success,' I replied in the repetitive custom of Chinese self-effacement.

'No, no, no, no, I wish you success.'

We were both grinning when the head referee waved for us to enter the arena. In *sanda*[1] tradition, fighters were expected to run out together to show their enthusiasm and mutual respect. As we started running, the Champ grabbed my hand, which was an extremely unusual show of solidarity – I'd never seen it done before, let alone experienced it. The crowd roared its approval. Looking back it strikes me that if only we'd started skipping, it would have been the gayest fighter's entrance in the history of combat sports.

On top of the platform we went to opposite sides to stretch. The Champ's splits were perfect, so despite my six-inch height advantage he'd be able to kick me in the head. I stopped glancing over at him.

As we approached the center of the ring, the noise of the crowd rose and the disparate shouts joined into a singular distinct voice crying two phrases over and over again in a steady drumlike beat:

Shale ta! (Kill him!)

Da si laowai! (Beat the foreigner to death!)

I shot a look over at Coach Cheng.

Once again my only anchor, he shrugged apologetically.

Amituofo[2].

To be fair, the crowd had no way of knowing I spoke Chinese. I'm certain if they had, they wouldn't have been chanting for my death. They would have been too self-conscious. But ignorant that I understood them, they kept at: *Beat the foreigner to death! Kill him!*

The referee explained the rules. The Champ and I bowed to each other and hugged. This time I kept my back straight.

When the bell rang, I could no longer hear the crowd.

We stood deathly still in the middle of the ring, neither one of us wanting to bounce or show any signs of anxiety. The pressure built. I felt compelled to move. I hopped

[1] *Sanda = Chinese kickboxing*

[2] *Amituofo = has several meanings. Here it means 'I'm sorry'.*

219

forward and back, feinting to see if he would react. He didn't. I feinted again and then took a bigger step forward with my left to close within kicking range, and launched a right roundhouse[1].

This is what the Champ was waiting for. He had correctly anticipated a kick. Without any wasted motion or doubt, he trapped my leg, ducking his head down, so I couldn't punch him in the face. And with a speed I'd never experienced before, the Champ dropped his left leg back and lowered his body, which pressed my leg away and downward. Before I knew it I was flat on my back with him standing over me.

2-0.

The catch and throw was so perfectly executed it intimidated me. I decided to switch from an offensive to defensive strategy and try to catch one of his kicks.

He shuffle-stepped forward and launched a left side kick aimed at my chest, which was about the level of his neck. I saw the kick coming, but it was too fast for me to trap it. I felt the impact before my mind was able to register the kick had landed.

4-0.

I was rocked back a step. No one, not even Baotong, had ever kicked me that hard. I remember thinking with astonishment, *That really hurt*, as I watched him repeat the attack. I tried to trap his foot again, and again I was too late. My breath blew out of my mouth as the force of his side kick pounded my sternum.

6-0.

We were in the dance now, and I was on the losing end of it. I knew I had to attack. I tried a side kick, but he blocked it downward with his right forearm, sending a jolt of pain up my leg as he stepped back and out of the kicking range.

Combinations!

I immediately followed the failed side kick with a right roundhouse. He hooked it to the side of his body, allowing the kick to connect with his left arm. My body tensed, preparing to be thrown to the ground. We were standing face-to-face. He placed his right hand on my chest, and then he started running forward. With only one leg to stand on, I was forced to hop backward to keep my balance. He was running me, like a wheelbarrow, off the platform.

As I reached the edge of the *leitai*[2], he let go of my leg and pushed with his hand against my chest. Flying through the air, the thought that flickered through my mind was: *That's not fair*. To prevent a wrestling match, the referee is supposed to stop any throw that takes longer than two seconds to execute. *That took longer than two seconds, hometown ref!*

[1] *Roundhouse kick = when the attacker sweeps his leg round in a semi-circular motion*
[2] *Leitai = fighting platform*

The air left my body as I landed on the foam padding below. I was staring up at the hundred-foot-high rafters. It felt like it took forever to stand up.

10-0.

I knew with a sagging dread that this round was over. The psychological impact on the judges of throwing your opponent off the platform was worth much more than the official four points. Unless I was able to knock him off the *leitai* in the next minute and a half, I'd have to win the next two rounds.

As I stepped onto the platform, the realization that he'd dropped me to the canvas, kicked me twice, and tossed me off the leitai in less than thirty seconds settled over me like a heavy weight. With absolute certainty I knew he was too good for me. There was no way I was going to win. As we faced each other again, I could hear these words bouncing around inside my skull: *Pride. Too good. Face. Coach Cheng. Pride. Deqing. He's too good. Pride. You're fighting for pride now.*

So I started to dance. I shuffled. I backpedaled. I circled around the ring using my longer arms and legs to keep him out of range. It wasn't Ali, but I was dancing. Shuffle. Punch. Backpedal. Shuffle. Kick. I had generalship of the ring, if only for a brief moment. In my head I was moving faster than in fact I was, but still I held the Champ off for the rest of the round. I'd closed the scoring gap but not enough: 20-10 was my best guess.

The five referees lifted their cards. They were all black for my opponent.

I'd lost the round but salvaged my pride.

But I wasn't thinking about that when I returned to my metal chair where Coach Cheng and Deqing were waiting for me between rounds. As I sat down, I didn't believe I would ever be able to stand up again.

Coach Cheng had my legs up on his knees, rubbing them. Deqing was pouring water into my mouth.

'Keep moving, you must keep moving,' Coach Cheng shouted at me.

I could barely hear him over the screaming crowd and buzzing in my ears.

'My legs,' I whispered.

'What?'

'My legs. They feel like cement.'

'*Mei Shi*[1]. Keep moving. Punch, kick, move.'

'I can't. My legs, they are so heavy.'

[1] *Mei Shi = no problem*

221

'*Mei Shi*,' Coach Cheng kept saying. 'No problem.'

It angered me. I wanted him to say it was okay. I'd done enough. I could quit now.

'I am so tired,' I said. 'I have never been this tired.'

Deqing grabbed my face. 'Remember what I told you before, 'It takes real courage to fight when all hope is gone.''

I nodded. But I didn't believe him.

It took both Deqing and Coach Cheng to pull me off the chair. I hated them for doing it. Couldn't they see how tired I was?

The walk to the *leitai* was the longest of my life. It felt like I was underwater. I slunk the ten feet to the platform with my head down. I had to brace my leg to step onto the platform.

I wasn't going to dance anymore. I didn't have the strength. And where's the pride in running? When the referee blew his whistle I charged. My side kick landed. I followed with a right haymaker[1]. The Champ ducked it. We rammed each other in the center of the platform. He had his hands around my waist. I grabbed him around his head. He lifted. I focused my qi[2] toward the ground, imagining my feet rooted to the center of the earth, as Coach Cheng had taught us. I couldn't let him break my contact with the *leitai*. He heaved. I held firm. The referee blew his whistle and separated us.

I attacked immediately. I felt wild, the last thrashings of a wounded beast. Left roundhouse to his leg. Right roundhouse aimed at his head. I needed to end this now.

He caught my right leg above his shoulder. My foot had connected with his face – two points – but it was trapped. He was carrying my leg like a log over his shoulder. He placed his right fist in my chest and started running forward. The endless, repetitive loop of a nightmare. I hopped backward until he launched me into the air.

That was longer than two seconds!

I was furious. I wasn't angry that the fight was for all practical purposes now over. I was in a rage that he had embarrassed me. Wounded my pride. All I could see was red. I was going to knock him off the damn *leitai* if that was the last thing I did.

At the first opportunity, I ducked my head and charged him like a linebacker, tackling him around the waist and driving forward with my legs.

He reached down and grabbed me around the waist as I drove him backward. It was the classic defense. You score four points if you throw your opponent off the platform

[1] *Haymaker = a punch using all the attacker's body weight*
[2] *Qi = energy flow*

222

while remaining on it, but if both fighters go over together, no points are awarded, no matter who hits the ground first. I knew he was going to pull me off the *leitai* with him. I didn't care. He was going off and I was going to land on top of him.

I drove to the edge with a shout. He went backward dragging me with him. In vain, I tried to remain on the platform. As I tipped over I decided to jump, so when he hit the foam, I could ram into him with as much force as possible. I even tucked my right shoulder so I'd strike with a sharper point.

I didn't see any visible signs of pain on his face. He was as placid as ever. The referee blew his whistle. No points. But the Champ was on his back, off the platform, and I was on top of him. That was victory enough for me.

For the last thirty seconds of the round, we danced around each other. He scored a few more blows than I did, but it was a formality. The fight was already over on the judges' card and in my mind.

The front cover photo of the special Wushu Festival edition of the Zheng Zhou newspaper showed me shaking hands and grinning with delight at the Champ from the silver-medal position on the top of the platform. The clear subtext was: 'Look at how happy the *laowai*[1] is to have had the chance to be defeated by a Chinese champion.'

In fact, at that moment, the list had popped up in my head.

THINGS THAT ARE WRONG WITH MATT

1. Cowardly

2. Boy/Not a Man

Getting back up on that platform and fighting a hopeless round was the bravest thing I'd ever done. I'd won by losing and in so doing accomplished the goal I'd set out to achieve at Shaolin. I was grinning at the Champ, because I'd finally found my courage.

Matthew Polly: American Shaolin (2007)

[1] *Laowai = foreigner*

A Question of Sport Activities

My Heroes Were Olympians

Before Reading

Scoring the Speech

As a class, you are going to imagine that you are members of the International Olympics Committee. As a committee member you will already know something about Sebastian Coe (see the fact box on page 225).

- Your job is to listen to Sebastian Coe's speech and to decide whether it persuades you to support the London bid. Does the speech persuade you that Britain is in tune with the 'Olympic spirit', in other words, the idea that sport can bring people together and inspire them?

- Listen as your teacher reads the speech. When she or he has finished, decide on a score out of ten for how persuasive you found the speech and some reasons for your score. For example, you might decide on a score of 8 because the story of Coe as a boy, watching the Olympics on television and becoming inspired to be an athlete, convinced you that London had really entered into the Olympic spirit.

- Listen as your teacher reads the speech a second time. This time, turn to a partner agree a score between you and be prepared to explain the score you gave.

- Share scores and reasons as a class.

Sebastian Coe Facts

Competed in the 800m, the 1000m and the 1500m.

During his career he held eight outdoor and three indoor world records.

He won four Olympic medals, two of them gold.

Served as an MP for the Conservative Party 1992-7.

Became a life peer in 2000.

———————————— After Reading ————————————

How Does the Speech Work?

1. Sub-headings

- As a class, read the first two paragraphs of the speech: 'Mr President, Mr Honorary Life President, Members of the International Olympic Committee, I stand here today because of the inspiration of the Olympic Movement.' Discuss what you think Sebastian Coe is trying to do in these paragraphs. For example, you might think he is introducing the fact that his speech is going to be a very personal one, or that he is reminding the Committee that he knows the Olympics from the point of view of an athlete.

- As a class, come up with a short subheading that would sum up what he is trying to do, for example, 'Coe the athlete' or 'Introduces personal point of view'.

- Read the next three paragraphs. Discuss whether these could be clustered under your subheading, or whether they are starting to do something different and would need a new subheading.

- Draw a chart like the one below on A3 paper and fill it in for the first four paragraphs. Leave the third and fourth column blank for now. You have been given some ideas to start you off, but you do not have to use them.

Cluster	Subheading	Persuasive techniques	My speech
Paragraph 1-2	Introduces personal viewpoint		
Paragraph 3-5	Coe's inspiration		

- Form groups of three. You are going to continue to read the speech and fill in the chart, discussing how to cluster the paragraphs and coming up with a subheading for each cluster, as you just did as a class. You should:

  - decide how to cluster the paragraphs according to what Coe is doing

  - as you decide how to cluster the paragraphs, come up with a subheading, which sums up what Coe is doing in each cluster.

- When you have finished, compare some of your ideas as a class.

2. Persuasive techniques

In his speech, Coe uses many of the features of effective persuasive writing. A few of the techniques he uses are listed below.

- Can you find an example of each in the text? When you find a technique, add a note in the third column of your chart, as shown in the example below.

Techniques for a Persuasive Speech

- **Anecdote:** this is the telling of a personal story. People tend to be more interested in other people than in lots of facts and figures so a personal story draws the listener in. An anecdote also shows that the speaker has personal experience of the issue.

- **Emotive language:** this is the use of language that is likely to stir up strong feelings in the audience. When you get people involved emotionally, they are more likely to listen to what you have to say. They may be quite moved by your speech and be more ready to believe what you say.

- **Direct address to the audience:** this is when the speaker uses 'you' as if they were speaking directly to one member of the audience. This is another technique to make the listener feel personally involved. The technique is often used with a bit of flattery – telling the listener how intelligent, kind or caring they are if they agree with the speech.

- **Repetition and listing:** when you read something you can re-read and look back, something you can't do with a speech, so repeating and listing words and ideas makes the key points stand out in people's minds.

Cluster	Subheading	Persuasive techniques	My speech
Paragraph 1-2	Introduces personal viewpoint		
Paragraph 3-5	Coe's inspiration	Anecdote	

Your Own Writing

A Persuasive Speech – Why You Should Give Us £3,000

You are now going to write a speech. You can do this on your own or in pairs.

■ Choose one of the situations below. In each situation you are trying to get a committee to agree to give some money for a project.

---

1. School improvements

The senior staff at your school have £3,000 to give away for a project that will improve the school for its pupils. The money will be given to the best project. You are going to make a speech to a senior staff meeting, explaining what you think the money should be spent on and persuading them that your idea is the best.

---

2. Better youth club

Your local council has £3,000 to give to your youth group, but only if you can persuade them that the money will be put to good use. You have been chosen to give a speech to the council persuading them that the money will be used well to improve the youth club.

---

3. Up Your Street

A television programme called *Up Your Street* offers £3,000 to groups of people living in the same area to complete a project that will improve life for local residents. You have to submit a speech on video to persuade the programme's producers to give money to your project. They will then choose the best one to be the subject of next week's programme.

■ Use your subheadings as instructions for what to do in each paragraph or cluster of paragraphs. For example, if you decided that in the first two paragraphs Coe was reminding the Committee that he knows the Olympics from the point of view of an athlete, in your first two paragraphs you are going to remind your audience that you have personal experience that has helped you to put together the best project. Use the fourth column of the chart to plan your speech before you write. An example is given below.

Cluster	Subheading	Persuasive techniques	My speech
Paragraph 1-2	Introduces personal viewpoint		Use youth club so know what is needed.
Paragraph 3-5	Coe's inspiration	Anecdote	How youth club helped my friend to stop getting into trouble.

227

The Voice Coach
Extension Work

In order to do this activity, you will need to have done the activities on 'My Heroes Were Olympians' on page 224.

'When we speak we always have enough breath to express a thought...'

1. Reading aloud

- With a partner, re-read the last three paragraphs of the text.

- In your pair, discuss what you think Stewart Pearce means when he says:

  'When we speak we always have enough breath to express a thought...'

- Now choose a section of Coe's speech (page 210) to re-read. Can you spot where each 'thought' ends? It will be helpful to use the punctuation of the speech as a guide. Read the section aloud, swapping readers at the end of each thought. Did you find you could fit each thought into a breath?

- Read the same section again, following some of the other instructions the voice coach gave Coe.

- With your partner, discuss what difference the instructions made and how difficult or easy it was to follow them.

2. Your own speech

- Look through your own speech. Practice reading it aloud and notice whether you can fit each 'thought' into one breath. If you find yourself running out of breath in some parts, try changing the way you have written these parts of the speech so that they are more comfortable and natural to read.

- Annotate your text with any instructions you think will be particularly important when you are reading it aloud, such as when to speak more loudly/quietly, quickly/slowly or with a particular tone of voice. Underline any words you want to particularly emphasise.

- Practice giving your speech to your partner. Feed back to each other to help you improve before giving the speech to the whole class.

Chin Up My Little Angel

Before Reading

Musical Chairs

■ Play a short game of musical chairs, then, as a class, discuss:

- What were people prepared to do to win? For example, cheat or push?
- What different feelings did people have about playing such a competitive game? For example, determined to win, or couldn't care less?
- How did the person who won feel? For example embarrassed, pleased?

Investigating an Extract

Jeremy Clarkson has for many years presented *Top Gear*, a BBC programme about cars. He is also interested in other forms of transport, machines and engineering. He is known for his sense of humour, his controversial and outspoken opinions and his lack of political correctness. He also loves word play, particularly similes and metaphors. For example, on reviewing a diesel car he commented: 'Sure it's quiet, for a diesel. But that's like being well-behaved... for a murderer.'

■ In pairs you are going to investigate one of the extracts below (your teacher will tell you which one to work on). For your extract you should:

- look up any words you don't know
- put the extract in your own words so that the rest of the class can understand the humour when they look back at the original.

My daughter is not sleek. In fact she has the aerodynamic properties of a bungalow...

She puts huge effort into running. Her arms and legs flail around like the Flying Scotsman's pistons but despite this you need a theodolyte to ascertain that she is actually moving forwards.

You could force your children to put the PlayStation away and stick to Monopoly, which has no winners and losers because nobody in the whole of human history has ever had the patience to finish a game.

It broke my heart when, as predicted, Emily was last in her running race, thumping across the line like a buffalo.

...arranging your face when you win is impossible. You have to look proud but magnanimous and that's hard even for Dustin Hoffman.

During Reading

Who is he talking to?

■ With a partner think about the audience Clarkson has in mind for his article. What phrases might describe them? You could use the prompts that follow to get you started.

  – Competitive people

  – People who are able to laugh at themselves

What's so funny?

■ Listen as your teacher reads the text aloud.

■ Listen to the text being read aloud again. This time your teacher will stop when she or he gets to an extract people have put into their own words. Listen to a few versions and discuss anything you still don't understand.

■ Pick any part of the text that you found funny and be prepared to explain to the class what you liked about it.

After Reading

Competition

■ Which of the following statements seems to best describe Jeremy Clarkson's attitude to competition? Discuss this with a partner, coming up with your own statement if you prefer. Find some words, phrases or sentences from the text that made you think this.

Competition is part of life so you might as well get used to it from a young age.	1
Adults are more competitive than children.	2
Losing is actually better than winning because at least you can make it into a funny story later.	3
Although we behave as if winning is important, we like losers better than winners.	4
Everyone likes to win. What's wrong with that?	5
Losing is awful and no-one should have to experience it.	6

Tournament

──────── Before Reading ────────

Losing

Have you ever been in a competition, a fight, an argument, or a game where you knew you were going to lose?

■ If you have, share your story with the class, explaining whether you kept going or gave up once you realised you couldn't win.

'You're fighting for pride now.'

■ With a partner, role play a short (serious) scene which contains the phrase 'You're fighting for pride now.'

■ Watch some of the role plays. As a class, discuss some of the different situations you came up with in which a person might 'fight for pride'.

'Face' – Cultural Context

You are going to read an extract from *American Shaolin* by Matthew Polly.

■ Before you begin, read the contextual information below.

- The Shaolin Temple is famous across the world as the birthplace of both Zen Buddhism and kung fu. Matthew Polly went there for two years to study martial arts with the Shaolin monks, well known for their tough training regime. During his stay Polly learned a lot about Chinese culture, including the importance of 'face'.

- The Chinese idea of 'face' is similar to what English-speaking people mean when they talk about 'saving face' or 'losing face' but it is also broader than that. It could be translated as 'pride', 'honour', 'respect' or 'good reputation'. In Chinese society it is considered very important to avoid losing face or causing someone else to lose face. There are lots of ways to increase 'face', for example avoiding making a mistake, acting in an honourable way, or receiving a compliment.

- When Matthew Polly fights in a kung fu competition, how he performs reflects on his 'face'. His performance can also reflect on the 'face' of his teachers, as it is a measure of their skill in teaching him.

──── During Reading ────

'I'd lost the round but salvaged my pride.'

- ■ Read as far as 'I'd lost the round but salvaged my pride'. **II**

- ■ Discuss as a class what is keeping Matthew going, even though he knows he will lose.

'I had to brace my leg to step onto the platform.'

- ■ Now read as far as 'I had to brace my leg to step onto the platform'. **II**

- ■ How does Polly get across how exhausted he is? With a partner, see how many different ways you can find, using the suggestions below to get you started. Discuss which technique you think is the most effective for putting across his tiredness to the reader.

    - – Repetition

    - – Using different senses

    - – A simile

'I'd finally found my courage.'

- ■ Now read to the end of the piece.

- ■ With a partner, and then as a class, discuss whether you think Matthew Polly was courageous. Use some examples from the text to back up your opinion.

──── After Reading ────

Boy/Not a Man

- ■ In his piece, Matthew Polly explores various linked ideas such as:

    - – what it means to be brave

    - – what it means to be a man, rather than a boy

    - – what it means to have 'face', or respect.

- ■ With a partner, discuss these ideas. Talk about what you think Matthew Polly is saying about each idea in his text, and whether you agree with him.

- ■ Share your points as a class.

——— Your Own Writing ———

Becoming a grown-up

■ Take ten minutes to think of three to five experiences in your own life where you had to behave like a grown-up, not a child. Make a few notes about each one. One of your experiences might be the story you told in the 'Before Reading' activity on 'Losing'.

■ Choose the most interesting experience. Tell your partner the story of what happened and how and why you had to be grown-up.

■ Write up your story as a piece of autobiographical writing. You could write about one experience or several. When you describe your experience, try to use some of Polly's techniques such as repetition, similes and using different senses.

Working with More than One Text

Comparing 'Chin Up My Little Angel' with 'American Shaolin'

For this work you will need to have read both 'Chin Up My Little Angel' and 'American Shaolin'.

■ If Jeremy Clarkson read Matthew Polly's piece, what do you think he might say about the way Polly thinks about competition and losing?

■ Imagine Clarkson writes Matthew Polly a letter explaining where he agrees or disagrees with what he has to say about competition and about losing. You could use some of the following phrases to help you write your letter if you wish:

I was interested in…

I really agreed with you when you said…

You're wrong about…

In my own experience…

I believe competition is important because… and you seem to think…

What I think about losing is… whereas you think…

Sports Day – a Class Debate

To do this activity you will need to have read 'Chin Up My Little Angel' and at least one other text from this section (not including 'The Voice Coach').

Imagine that the P.E department in your school has made a proposal:

'We believe that our school Sports Day should no longer be competitive.'

The department proposes that there will be various activities to take part in next Sports Day, but no winners or losers. (If your school already has a non-competitive Sports Day, imagine that the suggestion is to change it back to a competitive one.)

As a class, you are going to role play a meeting in which students, parents and teachers discuss and vote on whether to make the suggested changes to Sports Day.

1. Preparation in single role groups

■ Divide the class into groups, each taking on one of the following roles:

1. Students in favour of a non-competitive Sports Day.

2. Students who prefer a competitive Sports Day.

3. Parents in favour of a non-competitive Sports Day.

4. Parents who prefer a competitive Sports Day.

5. Teachers in favour of a non-competitive Sports Day.

6. Teachers who prefer a competitive Sports Day.

7. Observers who will be responsible for collecting ideas from different groups and keeping a note of them.

You will also need a chairperson who will be responsible for keeping the discussion in order and making sure plenty of people get a chance to contribute.

■ In your group you have 15 minutes to think of as many points as you can to support your point of view.

■ Before the discussion starts, each group should write a short statement explaining their point of view. Next choose a representative to read the statement aloud.

2. The debate

- Decide on a time limit for the debate.

- On the board, write up the proposal:

  'We believe that our school Sports Day should no longer be competitive.'

- The chairperson will read out the proposal to start the debate and then ask each group to read out their statement.

- The chairperson will then open up the discussion to the floor. This means that anyone can put up their hand and, if chosen by the chairperson, put forward their opinion. Even if you don't agree with the view you have been asked to represent, stay in role during the meeting. However, this could include changing your mind if the other side makes some particularly good points.

- The observers should make a quick note of any particularly good points on either side of the debate.

- When the time limit is up, or when people have run out of points, the chairperson should ask the observers to each feed back one or two key points from the debate.

- The chairperson will then take a vote of the number of people in favour of the proposal, and the number of people against.

—————— Your Own Writing ——————

Reporting the Meeting

- After the debate, write up the meeting as if you were a reporter for the local newspaper. You will find the notes the observers have taken very useful here. Either the observers could make a short presentation to the class of the key points they noted, or the teacher could photocopy their notes for everyone to use.

Text Types and Language Features

Writing to Inform

Audience: someone who wants to know about a topic.

Purpose: to provide information that is clear and easily understood, to share knowledge in an interesting and useful way.

Structure: logical, non-chronological, if appropriate, use layout and punctuation conventions such as subheadings and bullet points.

Some typical language features:

- Formal or informal tone depending on audience and purpose

- Selection of relevant facts and details. Examples and anecdotes to place information in 'real' contexts and keep the reader interested

- Present tense (unless writing about something that took place in the past)

- Usually impersonal and written in 3rd person but includes the writer's opinions.

Writing to Persuade

Audience: someone you are trying to convince or influence.

Purpose: to change the way someone thinks or acts, to advertise or market goods or services.

Structure: logical, non-chronological, usually a number of points supporting a single viewpoint.

Some typical language features:

- Past tense

- Personal pronouns to involve the reader (I, we, you, ours)

- Repetition and listing, often in groups of three

- Rhetorical questions

- Informal tone if appropriate

- Anecdote, humour, examples, emotive language as appropriate

- Persuasive connections such as surely, clearly, obviously, of course.

Writing to Argue

Audience: someone who is interested in an issue.

Purpose: to present a case for or against a point of view to convince the reader.

Structure: clear and engaging introduction, logically developed paragraphs, making a series of contrasting points and leading the reader to a definite conclusion.

Some typical language features:

- Present tense

- Formal tone

- Logical connectives such as consequently, as a result, therefore. Persuasive connectives such as surely, clearly, obviously, of course. Comparative connectives such as on the other hand, whereas, in contrast.

- Impersonal or personal, depending on task and audience

- Rhetorical questions

- Repetition

- Anecdote, humour, examples, emotive language as appropriate.

Writing to Describe

Audience: could be a personal record, or for others, depending on task.

Purpose: to communicate a feeling or experience, to create a visual image of a place, person, action or object, to create an effect on the reader.

Structure: mostly non-chronological.

Some typical language features:

- Adjectives and adverbs

- Powerful verbs

- Figurative language (similes, metaphors, personification) and the five senses

- Personal tone – personal perspective and feelings

- Past, present and future tenses for effect

- Can be imaginative or factual.

Writing to Advise

Audience: someone who wants recommendations, opinions or suggestions.

Purpose: to give guidance on a course of action, decision or choice.

Structure: logically developed paragraphs, blend of argument and persuasion.

Some typical language features:

- Shows an understanding of the reader's situation

- Could be formal or informal depending on task and audience

- Present tense (usually)

- Personal pronouns – address the reader directly

- Balance positive and negative points (on the one hand, on the other hand, whereas…)

- Examples e.g. of how others have dealt with a similar situation

- Suggestions sound attractive and easy to follow – reassure the reader

- Gives suggestions, not orders

- May include conditional phrases such as if…then…

Writing to Instruct

Audience: someone who wants to know how to use or do something.

Purpose: to tell people how to do or use something.

Structure: step-by-step, chronological (time) order.

Some typical language features:

- Verbs in the imperative (for example, 'mix in the butter' or 'switch on the machine')

- Present tense

- Impersonal

- Formal

- Often uses bullet points or numbered steps

- Chronological (time) connectives such as first, next, then

- May include conditional phrases such as if…then…

New Scientist Answer

In the dock

Why are dock leaves so effective at relieving stings from nettles? Are they effective on any other plant or insect stings? Is this how the name is derived?

Tim Crow
Highnam, Gloucestershire, UK

Being stung by a nettle is painful because the sting contains an acid. Rubbing the sting with a dock leaf can relieve the pain because dock leaves contain an alkali that will neutralise the acid and therefore reduce the sting. Bees and ants also have acidic stings so dock leaves should help, but other alkalis, such as soap or bicarbonate of soda, are usually better.

However, a dock leaf is useless against wasp stings, which contain an alkali. This is unfortunate because wasps are nasty little critters whose sole aim in life is to ruin picnics and barbecues. If you want to neutralise a wasp sting you should use an acid such as vinegar. The only problem is you'll smell of pickles for the rest of the day.

Peter Robinson
Liverpool, UK